AF269304

THE HIDDEN WONDER

The Hidden Wonder of Reality, Faith, and the Soul

Reflections on the Golden Era
of Vágtázó Halottkémek
(Galloping Coroners), a Hungarian Band

Translated from the Hungarian by Diana Senechal

Sándor Czakó

The Hidden Wonder of Reality, Faith, and the Soul
Reflections on the Golden Era of Vágtázó Halottkémek
(Galloping Coroners), a Hungarian Band

Translated from Hungarian by Diana Senechal

Copyright © 2026 Sándor Czakó

First Edition

Paperback ISBN: 9781947175754

All rights reserved. No part of this book may be reproduced or transmitted in any form or by any means, electronic, digital, or mechanical, including photocopy, audio recording, or any information storage and retrieval system, without prior permission from the publisher or author (except by reviewers who may quote brief passages). No part of this book may be used or reproduced in any manner for the purpose of training artificial intelligence technologies or systems. Any references to historical events, real people, or real places are used to the best of the author's memory.

Cover art and book illustrations by Géza Barcsik

Exterior formatting by Jacob Arms
Published by Serving House Books
Lawrence Landing Company
Raleigh, North Carolina 27609
United States of America

www.servinghousebooks.com

Serving House Books is a proud member of:

Independent Book Publishers Association
 and
Community of Literary Magazines and Presses

CONTENTS

The Hungarian title has a hidden acronym, VHK, which stands for the band's name, Vágtázó Halottkémek (in English: GC. or Galloping Coroners), which cannot be rendered in translation without distorting the meaning considerably. In addition, for the original Hungarian book, the author used the anagrammatic pen name Zàn Coaskòrd. The band is not named in the original text; to assist readers, it has been named here in the title and in the translator's foreword.

Translator's Foreword

Sándor Czakó's *The Hidden Wonder of Reality, Faith, and the Soul*—part memoir, part spiritual and psychological exploration—tells the story of the golden era of Vágtázó Halottkémek (Galloping Coroners), a Hungarian band that saw its heyday in the 1980s and remains legendary today. Ecstatic, spontaneous, visionary, their concerts gave Hungarian and international audiences an experience unlike anything they had known before. (The band has been praised by Iggy Pop, Jello Biafra, Henry Rollins, and others.) Focusing on the 1980s and delving into the band's history, practices, sound effects, and unique form of performance art, Czakó explores the principles underlying the miracles of these shows. With excursions into principles of hypnosis, relativity theory, and social critique, this volume gives the reader much to consider while also telling about a band and an era.

The book is not an advertisement; thus it names neither the band nor its members. In the original Hungarian edition, the author writes under a pen name, an anagram of his own name. In contrast, both the author and the band are named here, in the English translation. Hungarian readers quickly glean who the book is about; not only do book reviews mention this, but the band's initials, VHK, are encoded in the title. This cannot be accomplished in translation without considerable distortion of meaning; thus, English-language readers need more information from the start.

When I first read the book, it came to me as a joyous kind of elegy: a tribute to an era that is no more, along with an affirmation that some trace of it continues, through the life of the soul. Upon subsequent readings, and during the translation process, I was drawn into its underlying arguments and details, its combination of logic and intuition, and its spiritual and intellectual liveliness. There have been times, during reading or translating, when I felt as though I were at one of the concerts.

The book is not meant to be scholarly or scientific; its forays into psychology and relativity theory are speculative, intended to stimulate thought and raise possibilities. The author takes risks, just as the music did, drawing unexpected connections between subjects. Along the way, he brings up ancient transcendent knowledge, the particular wonders of the Hungarian language, ritual theater, sound effects, and the principles underlying hypnotic suggestion, while reflecting on the music and its era.

The Galloping Coroners' concerts were inherently life-changing in that each one was new. No one knew what a given concert would entail. As the author describes, the band members established certain "internal images" in advance but left their implementation to the inspiration of the moment. When the concert took off, the band members sensed and responded to each other and to the music, and the audience to all of this. Within a short time, amidst the shrieking, howling, leaping, and swinging, the drum rhythms, and guitar riffs, the effects, everyone was united in an overwhelming, instinctive experience of faith and love.

Until 2025, when VHK and Platon Karataev gave a concert together (for VHK's fiftieth anniversary and Platon Karataev's record release), I had never attended a Galloping Coroners show. I came to Hungary long after the original band's heyday (the band continues, but with a different lineup and atmosphere). Through these pages I could not only imagine the concerts but relate them to my own, quite different experiences of faith, immersion, and suggestion.

For those entirely unfamiliar with the band, the book provides links to a few online resources. While the recordings do not approximate the live experience of the shows, they can help readers glean what the latter may have been like.

I enjoyed this project, learned from it, and hope that it helps the book reach readers around the world. As the author writes in the Foreword, "A human loves to seek and find wonders." I have found wonders in this book; if I have conveyed some of them here, then my hopes have been fulfilled.

—Diana Senechal

Szolnok, September 2025

Acknowledgements

Many people and friends have influenced this book; I give them special thanks for the meeting of our life paths.

I am likewise grateful to my band-friends for living out[1], together with me, the enthralling and boundless freedom of our unbridled, adventurous youth; and originating a unique, spontaneous, suggestive, and free musical creative process, the band's singular and particular invention.

I am deeply grateful to Diana Senechal for translating this book with such care and intelligence, and for contributing an illuminating Translator's Foreword and explanatory footnotes. I also owe her special thanks for the generous intellectual support that accompanied and helped sustain the English-language edition.

I would like to express my greatest gratitude and love to my wife, Edit, who supports me in everything.

I thank Life for giving me my magnificent children and thus allowing me to dedicate this book also to Viktória and Sebestyén, who likewise supported me and whose ways of being inspired this writing.

---

[1] In the original Hungarian text, the author uses different words, each with its own nuance, to convey "living out," "encounter," "experience," and "empirical experience." In this book, the word *átélés* has two meanings: first, a "living out" of something, and second, a fully lived internal event or encounter that triggers a profound experience and inner transformation. The word *élmény* refers to an experience—that is, a lived event translated into memory and description; and the word *tapasztalat*, a concrete empirical experience. The translation cannot always render the distinctions between them, but in terms of the book's larger meaning, they are all important and present.

Foreword

A human loves to seek and find wonders.[2] Perhaps we sense that life holds much more for us than we realize at a given moment, more than we are capable of living out. Yet this natural longing of ours is suffocated by today's rushed life pace, the urge to conform to greedy, egoistic globalization. Still, experiencing this magic seems simple.

This book speaks of wonder: in particular, by explaining the magic that a Hungarian underground band left behind. It came about through a kind of performative music creation that they originated and brought to the surface, which offered a special spiritual, noetic experience of freedom and which perhaps arose instinctively at first, later more consciously.[3] Perhaps one can say that in the history of music, such suggestive, free creation, grounded in internal image-making and inducing a remarkable experience of spiritual identification, is the band's unique invention, of universal significance.[4]

Wonder actually lies dormant in the world and in us; we just have to find it, put it into action, and turn it into an effect.

Our lives and the world are full of simple beauty, perceptible by all. These are the kinds of wonders that many people take for granted and pass over, because to live these miracles fully, one needs a kind of internal, magical energy, which likewise lies hidden in everyone. This

---

[2] In the original Hungarian text, the word for "wonder" is *csoda*, which can also mean "marvel" or "miracle," and in its Slavic origins could even refer to a "thing." None of the translations of this word is perfect; "wonder" sounds too vague, "miracle" too confining, and "marvel" slightly maudlin. There is something tangible about *csoda*, perhaps deriving from its ancient origins.

[3] In this book, the word "noetic" (*szellemi* in Hungarian) is used in the sense of "relating to mental activity or the intellect."

[4] The phrase "belső képalkotás" can be translated as "internal image-making," "internal image-formation," or "internal picturing." It refers to the creation of images—including moving images—in the mind. After the first occurrence, this phrase will be translated as "internal picturing" for the sake of conciseness and flow. In any case, this refers to the mental creation of *new* images—albeit images that draw on lived experience and imagination.

source inside us allows us to live out that moment of magic, or rather, it allows us to notice, with childlike awe, those wonders of life that appear insignificant and tiny.

Such wonders might include listening to cathartic music or a performance, or similarly, taking in and experiencing a work of art; they include the radiance of a sunrise or the magic of a nighttime starlit sky, the voice of a bird or whale, and not least of all, a raindrop trickling down the windowpane, a teardrop rolling down a cheek, or a smile.

If our outer and inner worlds function properly and in unity, we are granted that spiritual balance and potential through which our lives can become fulfilled and lovable.

If we use this spiritual energy hiding within us for creation, we can experience its transformation into something powerful and enduring, that is, a wonder or miracle, because it can change reality—our faith—which in turn can change our lives and perhaps the world. We need only consider the marks left by ancient cultures on today's world.

I will try to reveal the path to this wonder by telling about an experience created and lived out by an underground band.

Introduction

I wrote this book as a founding member of a band, whose name, along with the names of its members, I intentionally am leaving unmentioned, just as I will not name the theater performance group or other individuals who collaborated with us. Since this coterie did not receive much media support at home, in the 1980s-90s or later, I thought that in this self-promoting celebrity world, I would provide the final touch with this tiny gesture. Yet it is possible that I will achieve the opposite. Regarding the passage of time, this ancient Mexican saying seems to hold true: "They tried to bury us, but they didn't know that we were seeds."

Nonetheless I think the readers will readily glean who this book is about. Despite the negative media campaign in Hungary, the band's activities, besides succeeding at home, met with appreciative responses in underground and other musical forums, primarily in Western Europe but also globally. Often, and in many different ways, people have tried and still try to categorize the band in terms of musical styles, but these attempts have always failed. In fact, we did not follow any musical trend; to the contrary, we chose a new, untrodden path, whose essence was the creation and conveyance of a particular spiritual experience.

The initial stimulus to write this book occurred when I came upon my old notes and memoranda, born when, after our successful concerts, I tried to interpret my particular experiences of music-making and sought to explain their effect on me. Here I try to combine those lines with my current insight and discuss the relations between them.

This work has a double foundation: my experiences in the band over several decades and the practical psychological experiences that I have processed in hindsight. With the help of these, I have attempted to delineate how the effective creative process is realized. My particular goal has been to shed light—primarily for the young generation—on those internal capabilities, the comprehension and development of our brain functions, which, when put to use, can open up new perspectives in our lives.

I must emphasize that in my many mentions of the band and—to be presented later in the book—the ritual movement theater, I speak exclusively of what took place in the 1980s; that is, the successes and attainments of that decade form the background of the book. For me, that era was the time when the band truly brought new and defining fundamentals into being and when it could offer the most moving concert experiences. The audience headcount also bore witness to this, as there were concerts with several thousand people in attendance.

In addition, I wish to stress that I did not intend this book as a scientific treatise, but rather as a literary work that shares and explains my lived experiences; for this reason I appended only a minimal bibliography. It was not my intent to refute or uphold the relevant scholarly stances and conclusions. Drawing conclusions from my own experience, I try to show the way to our internal paths and, in an unprecedented manner, to cast proper light on their mechanisms. After the years I lived out in the band, the experiences described in the book have matured in me; I have put them in words that reflect my perspective and interpretation. Naturally I sought out channels and information sources where I could look into the given topics; by reworking them, I came to formulate a picture of how our inner being works, which in this book I try to base on the imprint of my own artistic life. It was an internal prompting that suggested to me that this book might be worth writing, that it might be worthwhile to shed light on the fascinating mutual effects that form the relation between our internal spiritual energy and our brain function.

Over the course of our musical career, I was affected often, and in many ways, by trance states and hypnotic suggestion. At first we lived these experiences unawares, and then, more and more consciously, we began to heed them and interpret their workings as well as their magic powers. In the end, I decided to try to give a picture of these wonderful internal wellsprings as manifested in routine experiences. I believe that experience is both the most effective and the most natural way of gaining knowledge. I would like to stress that the conclusions and principles set down in this book do not necessarily coincide with the pertinent national and international scholarly positions, which I used along the way to supplement and explain my experiences. Moreover, scholarly literature in this field is divergent and contradictory.

I esteem the increasing receptivity of today's young people toward internal, archaic, and pure spiritual matters, as well as their need to live out boundless internal freedom, which gives birth to such energies in our souls and hearts as can be passed on to our other human companions. In our lives these are truly exciting adventures: the experience of our brain function and application, the discovery of our noetic resources, and the act of putting them to use. Perhaps these are the cornerstones that gave me a basis for sharing the noetic and spiritual experiences of twenty or so years in the band, synthesized through my perspective and offered here as a special key, a useful and life-shaping legacy.

To better convey the need for a sincere, unmanipulated world, free of human trickery—which is increasingly prevalent—I will briefly give a picture of those retrograde forces that steer individuals in a negative direction. Interestingly, these manipulated negative forces use precisely the same source that this legacy holds, but perhaps in spite of this, once we illuminate its essential working, we can receive the proper strength and motivation to move our lives and human relations along a positive course.

In this book I will introduce, many times and in many forms, the adaptation and workings of archaic transcendent, magical knowledge; this may seem repetitive, but I do it to facilitate better understanding and more vividly draw attention to the dormant presence in all our lives, which needs only a spark to expose its effect and break forth like an avalanche. Several times in the book I bring up and explain the internal events of internal picturing and hypnosis, in several forms, not always in the same way, as I try to illuminate the workings of these psychological and internal mechanisms in different terms, through different relations. In a similar way we experience our everyday lives: minutes, hours, days, and years repeat themselves, perhaps following monotonously upon each other, yet when we live out and perceive the magic of a celebratory moment, the routine of our lives can become different and thus more interesting and full.

In each person's life there may come a moment when he feels the overwhelming force of love, or perhaps that heavy weight that the soul has to bear when it loses a loved one. These are good examples of the essential spiritual activities that can reach us in our everyday lives. Through these, everyone can feel the extraordinary impact of a spiritual event or encounter. This feeling is completely different from everyday joy and hurt, since it can affect and shock us much more deeply.

I will try to give a more precise, more process-oriented definition and explanation of artistic activity through a deeper exploration of our inner working mechanisms.

We have the capacity to induce a profound spiritual encounter and cathartic experience in ourselves and others. Some realize this capacity unconsciously, but we can consciously strive to appropriate this boundless energy source and use it to expand the possibilities of our lives. I consider this book an innovation in that, in its own way, it points to the possibilities of human brain function according to the theory of special relativity. With this, perhaps I have succeeded in finding the path and bridge between our cognition and thoughts as described and analyzed through scientific approaches, as well as through transcendent approaches and experiences for whose management and interpretation we must cross our everyday boundaries.

The magic of a given moment arises from the effect that our soul conveys and transmits to our consciousness. We can reach this effect by gaining and using ancient transcendent knowledge. In the following pages I will attempt to lay out this process in detail.

Manipulated Mass Hypnosis:
Its Influence on the Consciousness[5]

In every area of life, whether science or culture, it is evident that in a turbulent world we are losing the capacity for sustained attention. We outsource more and more information: that is, our smartphones and computers are available around the clock, so we retain less and less in our brains. Thus our knowledge shrinks, and our brain use and recall are pushed to the background. This sense of eternal availability, suggested by the external, controlled modern world, gives us a false illusion of mastery. It tricks us into deeming ourselves possessors of all knowledge, when in fact we only know the surface of things.

With the development of information technology, we face an increasingly immense information deluge. One result of this, among others, is that we often divide our attention among multiple matters. Given the abundance of data, we wish to stay abreast of everything that is going on around us, all the information at our disposal. We satisfy that urge instinctively by having everything on the internet available immediately and at all times. Virtual cloud services enable us to fill our "artificial brain," which serves as a repository, with all sorts of mementos of our past: pictures, music, important notes, events we have lived through, future projects, deadlines, deep or cursory study material that we still value, or other items we do not wish to store in our own brains. By thus freeing our brains of information, we can deal strictly with the present and what we need to accomplish within it. Thus, more and more, our brains start to neglect not only the deep knowledge and basic familiarity acquired through study, but matters of the past and future. Thanks to information storage technology, concrete, immediate matters take precedence, and our brain capacities give them priority.[6]

---

[5] In this chapter, when discussing the forces that influence the consciousness, I deliberately do not associate them with any particular individuals or groups. The pertinent forces are not necessarily consistent, coordinated, or unified, yet they have similar goals (wealth, power, control) and thus similar strategies and techniques.

[6] Philip Zimbardo.

As a result of this hypnotic suggestion, the outer world becomes inessential to us: people, our friends, our family and other relationships, their celebrations. A long time ago we made note of our loved ones' birthdays; now it is superfluous to do so, since they are stored by "Big Brother," who hides behind a cloud and watches us surreptitiously. Our brains adapt to quick bursts of information, and in parallel with this, we lose our capacity for more immersed thought. The more we have to divide and constantly fragment our attentions, the less capable we become of experiencing deep internal feelings. Since we have lost archaic behavioral and relational bonds, our emotions no longer function as well, and our relationships suffer. Beyond this, our knowledge of the affairs and workings of the world, of essential interrelationships and their creative application, recedes more and more. This sly, brain-invasive process can be understood as a kind of influence, which egoists and hedonists cultivate in various ways and which bombards us with hypnotic suggestion.

This process invisibly and slyly destroys the relation between humans and nature, as well as the pure relations between humans, based on societal norms, that have existed and refined us since ancient times. This type of manipulated mass hypnosis is one of the most dangerous weapons against humanity today. It nullifies one of society's most fundamental constructive forces: our direct relationship with our human companions. By imperceptibly infiltrating the consciousness, it destroys nations and their cornerstones, families. Today's emergent youth no longer connect with traditions that have existed for millennia. Through mass hypnosis, the broad masses are offered the "best" products again and again in new, shiny coating—products whose warranty no longer matters. As the world works today, products with preset lifetimes can no longer be repaired, since they have been designed to stop working after the warranty has passed. As a result, service companies and ventures have gone out of business. The only solution is to throw away the obsolete product and buy a new one. It seems that the goal is to nurture mindless, self-serving purchasing power. This line of force traverses the entire world, affecting everything from education to economic and political life to art, and thereby human beings, but most of all youth, who otherwise yearn for new things grounded in genuine truth. We should realize that our consciousness is being manipulated.

Thanks to this and other causes, in today's western society the ego rules, hedonism has become fashionable, and deceitful self-images distance people from the earth's reality, from nature, and from true and substantial relationships with others. Most people have come to equate the convenience of idolized money with happiness; because of this, they prefer the superficially familiar to the true and profound, and place their own interests first.[7] According to a well-known saying, "The ego is the worst confidence trickster we could ever figure, we could ever imagine. Because you don't see it."[8] The problem is that the ego is hiding right inside us. Today, as a result of mass hypnosis incited by advertising campaigns, everyone seeks self-fulfillment; however, in doing so, they gradually weaken the ancient cohering power of family and friendship. As a result, women today waste away in singledom, men as rowdy hedonists in well-tailored suits, filling their days with decisive action, and neither one enjoys the virtual world's false and superficial magic, which claims more and more space. Wordless people staring at their gadgets in their vehicles and on the street are trying to live out their virtual and distorted world.

Western cultures and ways of life, influenced by the media, try to stifle people's critical sense, as well as all their forms of recognition. Our language and media images are already ensnared by this reality-excluding mechanism, whose special hypnotic suggestions influence how we perceive what is happening all around us. Adapting to this, people have invented a kind of discrete language and communication, which they use to isolate themselves from the truth. We can find evidence of this in all commercials and promotions. Western culture and media convey a confusing and unsatisfactory reality, full of distorted facts and ideals. Someone could also perceive positive incentives here, but for one thing, these fabricated images are ungrounded and unrealistic and thus conducive to disappointment; for another, the messages they convey are self-serving. Yet this process has become so habitual that the average person fails to see that its images are not true to life but rather false, illusory, manipulated representations.

---

[7] Philip Zimbardo
[8] Dr. Yoav Dattilo

Let us consider what would happen if our kings and queens of old, representing great and noble ideals, were to come to life today. For instance, how would they grapple with the fact that today a well-known, world-class football player brazenly demands a great sum of money relative to the salary of a scientist who solves world issues and problems and propels our lives forward? Or let us compare it to the appreciation that teachers receive for instructing the younger generations. To make matters worse, gold-throated speakers suavely and smilingly publicize this fact as though it were the most natural thing in the world. It would also seem strange to them that criminals can become media entertainers, or that reality shows and self-promoting celebrities can broadcast falsehoods rather than reality.

Why do we keep polluting our external and mental environment, even knowingly, and what might the fatal consequences be? Clearly the resultant profit, as well as entanglements and ever-encroaching corruption, defeats common-sense arguments and facts. Why is the viewer misled with false information in contests where the winner is already determined? Such forms of manipulation are an integral part of today's mass media, yet the program editors hide and direct from behind the scenes, serving negative forces. These facts draw attention to the serious manipulation of our consciousness, entirely contradicting logical arguments of common sense and advanced thought. For this and other reasons there is a great need in our world to bring forth and nurture a generation capable of sensing and handling the forces influencing the consciousness.

Perhaps a simple and slightly polarized metaphor—a version of Plato's Allegory of the Cave—could illuminate some of the workings of the manipulated forces affecting our consciousness. This model appears at several levels of society. Let us imagine a puppet theater, where the children reverently watch the performance, sometimes crying, sometimes laughing. The puppets play out the piece, and the children associate good and evil with them. But in fact it is the puppeteers who bring the puppets to life and move them, unseen, in the background. Thus the children indirectly become the puppeteers' mediums through the direct manipulation of the puppets. The forces directing today's world have been avoiding conflicts very cautiously up to now, while it is still possible, and like "excellent puppeteers" manipulate people's consciousness in the background, for which they use quite elegantly fashioned puppets. Of course these puppets can also be humans in the flesh, perhaps entirely unaware of the game, since they believe that they are the specially chosen, the custodians of power. They play their roles like primary mediums; thus, those directing them from behind the scenes cause them to believe that they are acting on their own. In the auditorium, ordinary people follow the events like secondary mediums. They too are caused to believe by the performed "fairytale" that they themselves are in charge of their fates; that they live, for instance, in a resplendent, free democracy, where people can fulfill themselves and their ideals. This image is quite believable and real, if only because both good and bad appear in it. That is, in accordance with logic, everyone can find his place in it, and their divergent views can clash if necessary.[9]

Empirical experience aside, research suggests that in our time it is societal opinion that defines success, not objective accomplishment or an achieved result. This explains why the manipulation of humans, mass suggestion, plays such an important role. It is no accident that every government coming to power takes control of the media and can thus manipulate the masses. But such manipulation is not restricted to the government. We know from experience that, in large shopping centers, the music playing in the background at restaurants and other public areas is so unqualifiedly bland that this itself is almost disturbing. I have no intention of exposing and revealing precisely how this blandness mechanism works. I just draw attention to its soul-crushing effect. This intention becomes even more apparent when we consider the increasing popularity in mass media of easy-listening, easy-watching programs compared to high-quality ones. Thus, alas, it is manipulated shows, not objective facts, that guide societal opinion.

Today's manipulated media world exploits the internal experiences brought about through internal picturing and leads people by the nose. It influences the human brain by triggering it directly, through a virtual world, with the aid of television, computer, and smartphone. This image creation, not realized internally, manipulates and stimulates a false

---

[9] In using this puppet theater metaphor, I do not associate the puppeteers—as politicians sometimes do—with any particular group, nation, or political orientation or subscribe to any conspiracy theory. I mean only to draw attention to the invisible manipulation in our economic, political, and daily lives.

internal event; moreover, this distorted ideal based on comfortable, familiar, unremarkable things produces supreme purchasing power. Another deadly effect of media and information technology is the promotion and encouragement of addiction, especially among the young generation. In fact, today's informatics and media destroy the internal picturing capabilities that we are born with. They atrophy the brain function that performs the internal image associations. For instance, television, offering the possibility of an image, immediately shuts off brain activity in this direction and projects a set of images that our brains did not create. This tendency also kills our soul, pushing its energizing quality into the background. Consider, in contrast, the power of authentic folktales spread by word of mouth and their educational influence over the centuries.

The soul is a pure resource within us, whose energy potential weakens at that very moment when our brains try to rule over others—that is, when we want to subdue or control them by controlling the ego. To avoid manipulating or being manipulated in this way, we must become aware of our spiritual and cerebral functions.

Soul-killing Noetic Traps

In the course of everyday thinking and learning, the facts and concepts we acquire are stored in our brains as a body of knowledge organized into a filing system, and our rational thought makes use of their combinations. We receive them, almost automatically, from the various compartments of the brain and apply them to our everyday lives. Surprisingly, in today's elementary and secondary schools, students are usually given a single key to the solution of a given problem. Even today, a creative approach to complex and multifarious solutions has not really gained ground. Without this, nothing compelling can be built from these items stowed away in mental files; nothing sends chills down the spine, no true, startling creation can come into being. You can forge lovely logical links out of our rational knowledge, but these crumble into worthless sand and scatter. You can bring beautiful sounds out of expensive, flawless instruments without undergoing any inner transformation or spiritual encounter, but this will produce no real effect, just pretty, soulless background music.

These examples are related to our brain functions: that is, the distinct roles of our cerebral hemispheres greatly influence our activities.[10]

The brain's left hemisphere is rational and logical. It analyzes all incoming information, works with hypotheses, and plans and executes the individual steps of problem-solving. It perceives time; it is critical and objective. Here is the nexus that processes linguistic signs (it interprets words) and creates sentences according to learned rules. The left hemisphere's workings are given preference and priority today in our usual practical life and education.

The brain's right hemisphere is creative, visual, and intuitive. It tends toward the arts, perceives music and melody, and handles singing and composing skills. It assists spatial vision, the recognition of colors,

---

[10] The following discussion of left and right hemispheres is not meant to be exhaustive. The connections between the parts of the brain are complex, and we are continually learning about them; nonetheless, recent research continues to point, with increasing nuance, toward distinctions between the hemispheres.

faces, and shapes. It does not understand discussion and cannot speak. Its emotional reactions are stronger; in a discussion, it senses the emotional nuances. It has no sense of time.

From the above discussion it is clear that our current world prioritizes the brain's left hemisphere, while in our everyday lives the right hemisphere goes to waste. Unfortunately, the era does not encourage change in this regard. In fact, the current IT trend—the storage of the largest possible dataset in the smallest possible data carrier—gives young people a false sense that they possess all knowledge. The information resides in an alien virtual space that we own, and not in our brains; we can access it at any time, like a supplementary brain, but it isn't really ours. A key repercussion is that we reduce the use of our left hemisphere as well, thereby depleting its storage and synthesizing capabilities.

In sum: the false sense of knowledge produced by today's information flow originates from our tendency to associate acquired information with understanding. That is, a person who "cannot see the forest for the trees," though armed with a smartphone, still will not be able to design a bridge or perform a heart surgery; if he looks up these topics on the phone, it will not help. Engineers and doctors do not perform their work according to smartphone instructions. We must see and grasp that the learning process cannot be omitted. Through learning, we can train our brains to activate our left and right brain hemispheres and make the most of the relation between them. The more areas of knowledge we manage to amass through learning, the more possibilities we give our brains to generate intuitive sparks. It is perhaps fortunate if a person can learn as much as possible in a way that puts the left and right hemispheres equally to use. The experience of the intuitive and rational approaches should be an important element of a person's life. To understand the world's affairs and workings more completely, we must strive, through learning, to acquire the kind of knowledge we can apply.

There are three primary steps to the process of learning. The first is when we understand what something is about: that is, when we can perceive and follow its logic and coherence.

The second step is acquisition, when, making the given material our own, we place it in our brains through pictorial or other means, so that we can later recall it with ease. Here the synthesizing skill comes into play, where we process the knowledge acquired from different sources by seeking their interrelations.

The third step is practice at the level of application, when, employing our right hemisphere, we mentally enable ourselves to apply the acquired body of knowledge, so that we can combine it with our internal matter and intuitions to create something new.

Educational and scientific practice, employing the left hemisphere's rational and logical thought processes, reworks knowledge gained from empirical observation and experience by systematizing it according to logical criteria and seeking its interrelationships. Drawing upon these criteria systems, we bring new definitions into being and explain additional phenomena. With this expansion of our understanding, an ever larger knowledge set is at our disposal, and we use it as needed to lead our lives. This process, pointed at narrow and specific goals, ends up narrowing rather than broadening our thought.

A key feature of the instantly accessible, capacious, and ever-increasing knowledge set is its continual atomization. Individual fields are becoming more and more specialized: a problem that one person would have solved in the past is now tacked by several, each of whom can complete only parts of it. Thus, the oversized jobs and projects grow cumbersome; because of external constraints, the work teams lack the capacity to complete them. One important repercussion is that intellectuals and professionals have less and less time for complex thinking and problem-solving, as well as for paying attention to each other, coming into spiritual contact with each other. This process leads to alienation and atomized human relations; over the longer term, it results in the disintegration of nations, and beyond that, a loss of identity. To understand the world and truly live in it, complex insights are indispensable. Since complex problem-solving is increasingly relegated to the background, the sharp separation of individual fields of knowledge leads to an increasingly paradoxical result, which in some cases takes the following form: a positive accomplishment in one field induces a much more dangerous, negative effect in another.

To solve the problems arising from environmental pollution in today's civilization, or to discover new energy sources, we need complex and creative approaches generated by internal intuition, yet public education systems around the world fail to serve this end. To the contrary, it seems that schools increasingly favor drudges from whom no creative and complex thought is required.

The world's directed political globalization efforts are at odds with current global professional and scientific approaches and activities. That is, we find that in scientific life, fields of knowledge are more and more atomized, and professionals' global and complex thought is dying out. One particularly destructive repercussion is that it has become common to employ the fashionable sort of managers who want to run a business without knowledge of the given area of work. Thus, for example, it is not unusual for a manager with a degree in the humanities to try to lead an industrial company without even rudimentary knowledge of this technical field.

Ever narrowing is the circle of those gifted with such thorough and comprehensive expertise that they can think on a broader spectrum and make use of their inner-intuitive, free-winged creativity. International political, economic, and financial cartels, acting in their own self-interest, yoke the pure innate workings of the true human soul and the faith radiating from us. These political and economic forces have been increasingly appropriating complex visions; to achieve their own financial aims, they have been destroying the creativity of the masses emerging from the citadels of science, while leveraging the expertise of those in their own spheres of interest for the sake of their goals.

According to a famous paraphrase of Einstein's words, "The intuitive mind is a sacred gift and the rational mind is a faithful servant. We have created a society that honors the servant and has forgotten the gift."

Our Hidden Resources

In childhood everyone has strong intuitive capability; for instance, small children live out a relationship with their favorite teddy bear. Actually, it is the game itself that everyone encounters and lives out internally at that stage. This game-life finds innate, almost automatic support in a powerful internal picturing capability (imagination), which at that stage still has strong and deep manifestations. If, when a child is immersed in his game, we throw his teddy bear out the window, he will immediately start sobbing; he believes so deeply in his internal image that connects him with the bear that, if startled out of this world, he might stay upset for a while. The situation is similar with fairytales, which, through the children's internal picturing, assist a profound internal event through which children believe the tale and almost live in it, become transformed by it. For a child it is especially easy to fall into an altered state of consciousness: small children react especially sensitively to hypnosis and engage easily and completely unconsciously, almost instinctively, in self-hypnosis as well. They listen rapturously to the same tale again and again. Moreover, the tales—and especially Hungarian folktales—exert their effect as magical text. Our ancient Hungarian children's tales relate the happenings of the universe and project them into our world. Our ancient legends always set down the events of the universe and play out in the cosmos, the empire of infinite time and space. In Hungarian folktales, with the first sentence, "Once there was, where there was not,"[11] the hypnosis takes off with suggestion, and is later strengthened by the repetition of actions, enhanced by magical fairy-tale numbers, sweeping the children "beyond the beyond" (literally, "beyond seven times seven countries"), where the "three brothers" strive with the "seven-headed dragon." The number three is generally mentioned in connection with the performance of magic deeds; the number seven, in

---

[11] The Hungarian equivalent of "Once upon a time" is "Egyszer volt, hol nem volt," or literally, "Once there was, where it was not," a paradox suggestive of a magical world.

táltos belief fables and treasure tales.[12] With these suggestions, the hypnotic effect deepens progressively, so that with the final sentence, "Here's the end, run with it!" the hypnosis's magic can break, thus resolving the cathartic experience and creating, in the child's dream that follows, the foundations of a new fairytale journey, which seals the experiences of the previous images.

When we become adults, we lose this instinctive capacity emanating from the soul. To be exact, modern civilization kills this spiritual force, which could otherwise energize our pure noetic resources. In fact, it has become common practice to push our right hemisphere's activity continually into the background. We live in a world of mass products; this impacts spiritual activity as well. Slowly and imperceptibly we regard and treat our human companions as mass products too. The soul is not a mass product, and a soulless human loses his intuitive capacity and creativity, as well as the feeling and radiation of love.

We live in a world of massive information flow where, despite the fact that the world has become more transparent and knowable, we still are unable to handle the terrible effects of this. Among other things, consider the impact that an avalanche-like information set might have on migration: photos, maps, messages, and other data vividly suggesting a better future in another country or part of the world.

But there is another important element that we should consider: the development of a mindset that can effectively process the atomized and ever-growing information set. This involves an extension of our brain function that does not shy away from the experience of infinity and the stretching of our scientifically established limits.

Why, then, is media dangerous, given that it works with pictorial, virtual, and informatic principles? On the one hand, precisely because it inhibits humans' innate internal picturing capacity by replacing it: it pushes out the intuitive brain function, and thereby depletes creativity's driving force. On the other hand, because it stops direct communication between humans, that spiritual force field which, realizing faith and spiritual encounter, enables the flow and image transfer of internal experience. Communication through media is never as strong or effective as real-life contact, yet by excluding direct relations, it can manipulate.

---

[12] In Hungarian mythology, a *táltos* is a person with supernatural powers, similar to a shaman.

Music heard on the radio does not offer an experience as great as live music. Although one can be misled by the excellent sound quality, the power that allows for a profound spiritual encounter and inner transformation is sadly absent. For this to come into existence, one needs people, soul, and an appropriate medium, which together create the atmosphere.

There are signs that alongside mechanical music and its attendant mass entertainment, live music is again on the rise among the young. In fact, "unplugged" concerts can draw large crowds. This suggests that young people—as well as people of every age—demand live music and performances and thus show disinterest in soul-destroying productions with commercial motives and false idols. But unfortunately this is true for an ever shrinking subset of creative youth.

According to psychological interpretation, hypnosis is a particularly altered state of consciousness, in which the participating individual's or group's self-regulating function diminishes, attention is rearranged, and one becomes capable of intensified fantasy with the help of internal picturing. While hypnotized, people examine external reality less than in their waking state, and thus are more tolerant of sustained distortion of reality. Their susceptibility to suggestion grows.

Independent of our conscious decision, hypnosis is present in and inextricable from our lives, even if millions of people's lives roll along without their ever realizing how often and in what situations they have received and lived out hypnotic suggestions.

That is, we experience hypnosis almost daily, we ourselves and our companions, individually or in a group. We are under hypnosis when we undergo such a profound experience, when watching a play or listening to classical music, that we become dulled to external stimuli. On such occasions our sense of time changes, we don't sense its passage, we don't hear external, disruptive voices or noises, so that sometimes we wake up only after repeated calls; to such a degree have we succumbed to suggestion and the effect of internal pictures. The situation is similar at a concert where young people move to the music obliviously, in a trance, and together live out the combined effect of the music and the beat. Or at a magic show. Such experiences can happen during relaxation or active alertness, depending on how and in what form the suggestions arrive.

At its essence, hypnosis's true goal and purpose is for a love relation, based on faith and paired with positive spiritual experience, to come into being and grow stronger. If someone becomes attractive to us, then a positive suggestion already acts on behalf of the other and can later become mutual. When hypnosis is enacted, its condition is mutual acceptance and faith in something, a profound trust in each other, and a mark of some common goal which, regardless of the situation, can only be positive and prospective. This can set off relaxation, relieve our fears and pains, intensify the force of the internal "I," or catalyze other positive energy. Thus both the giver and the receiver of the suggestion are involved in the hypnosis as participants and partners. This process turns into positive energy because we wish to convey some beautiful and noble effect through suggestion. Giving is always a noble thing, if it comes from within us, if we do it with our soul. It is often said that it is better to give than to receive. Giving is indeed an important milestone in the process of hypnosis. Suggestions can have destructive motives as well, we can recognize these through familiarity with our internal spiritual function, to the extent that we pay attention to it. Such experience that fills our soul with joy and evokes love has surely come about through purely motivated suggestion.

In the previous pages I sketched the importance and role of hypnosis activated through suggestion because in my judgement, during our band's activity, experiences created in altered states of consciousness played a decisive role. These experiences shed light on a hidden and still not entirely known area of our brain function. Somewhere inside us the soul's infinite, pure source and energizing capacity resides. I will try to map this out in a unique way.

The Band

It began in Budapest in 1972, when we lived under a "people's republic" form of government and tried through our rebellion, within the socialist thought current, to maximally inconvenience those who disparaged our activities. We did not do this consciously; our limitless desire for freedom and our need to liberate our original internal forces stretched the limits established by the system at the time.

Starting in adolescence, my strange spiritual sensory system took shape, which included extreme, large-scale reactions to internal experiences. Actually, I think this is true for every teenage youth who tests his wings and stretches limits. This meant that, on the one hand, I could react dynamically to cathartic experiences; and on the other, I became responsive to subtle and sensitive matters. My childhood classical music training, spanning more than ten years, also contributed to this, enabling me to live out my inner experiences keenly, over a broad spectrum.

Naturally I received a great impulse and enthralling experience directly from my bandmate friends. At the start of our teenage years, we were unbridled and unrestrained. After graduating from elementary school, one boiling September day, I was heading over to the high school year-opening ceremony, when a cream-blond athletic boy rushed across the road. Even then his intriguing and decisive character stood out among many unfamiliar boys and girls. He became the band's drummer. His exceptional sense of rhythm, combined with his practical attitude, quickly brought his outstanding talent to the surface. In high school we were already playing music in various formations and gaining a sense of the emotional radiation and cathartic experience of instinctive music-making. At the time I still didn't know that he, I, and another true friend would found the band. On first impression this other kid was quite a strange figure when I glimpsed him carrying a plastic bag, wearing a long white balloon coat. He radiated an intriguing self-awareness, a peculiar internal freedom, and a special personality. Behind his strange restraint, he projected unbridled and limitless liberty, coupled with serious intelligence. He became the singer as well as the text-and image-creator, and I the rhythm guitarist who also regularly sang.

The band is ignored by Hungarian media even today, even though it had many forums around the world. A book about it appeared, as well as a film that showed its activity; for this reason I do not wish to repeat the stories. I only wish to point out to today's younger and older people the possibility of such hidden, forgotten mobilization of energies which, once in our possession, allow us to awaken to the chance of a fuller and truer fulfillment of our lives. Perhaps the most important gift of this legacy is an attempt at ordering our foundation stones of thought about the world, and spreading this thought and applying it to today's conditions by effectively harmonizing our brain function and inner energies.

Perhaps the following discussion will allow us to view some of our everyday matters and lives in a different context, highlighting the importance of our social relationships, the power of love, and the soaring realized through profound experience, with which we can place our lives, souls, and worldviews on sure foundations. I believe that the meeting of our trio was an amazing and fateful moment that catalyzed the entire adventure that followed. The band's actions were guided by four simple but noble principles: friendship, sincerity, faith, and freedom.

It was enthralling to experience the manifestation of sincere friendly love, which became the mainspring of the band's entire work and functioning. We knew each other's spiritual and emotional resonances to the depths; our complete trust in each other made this possible. The striving for limitless spiritual and noetic freedom, and the faith, originating in our joint force and soaring through our musical productions, raised the band to the skies.

We glided between cloud-borne desires and fabulous dreams and wanted to live them all out, all with overwhelming energy. Our friendship enclosed us in a seemingly impenetrable shell, which multiplied us as an impressive force, and thereby gave the band a positive spiritual radiance that amazed not only us, but our fans.

The music we made arose through our sudden unification with it, in the moment. This unification was a bold undertaking that gave sure wings to spiritual freedom in the realm of happenstance and endless chaos.

For me, the band's heyday spanned the period from its founding to the mid-1980s. In retrospect, that was when truly definitive and lasting events occurred. That was when the power and magic worked in full glory and made the team into something cultlike.

The Initial Period

In Hungary between 1970 and 1980, the only bands that could officially perform were those that had received permission through the ORI (National Organizing Agency), after undergoing censorship. Texts were closely monitored; the music and performance style were also affected. We did not apply; this was not even a question. The existing bands were all so-called "subsistence" ensembles, that is, they mostly lived off of their music. However, this meant that they had to bow to their employers. That was the only way they could perform, release albums, receive publicity, or have their songs played by the media.

We had no desire to be part of that system of cogs and wheels, and we weren't capable of it. In accordance with our teenage, unbridled way of thinking, we wanted to redeem the world; we wanted to play music that had not yet been played in Hungary or anywhere else. We played music because we felt good in our skin; we stormed ahead and enthralled each other. We believed more and more in ourselves, in our friendship, and, along with that, in the unique music that we created together.

Our drummer's inimitable panache and exceptional sense of rhythm, apparent to everyone, gave definition to our music. He had a remarkable drumming style as well as a dynamic and ferocious beat. Our singer's persuasive, tranced performance style, movements, and singing (to uncommon lyrics) were enthralling. Likewise, our bassist's charismatic individuality had great impact and appeal; especially in the improvisational passages, he brought the best form and energy. Our solo guitarist soared, flawlessly fitting startling, dissonant, yet appropriate guitar runs to the music.

It became clear early on, from the start, that it wasn't enough to play, point for point, songs that had been written by others in foreign countries; we had to add something that came from inside us. We started to stretch the boundaries of songs we had practiced before, with freer improvisation. We found that these improvisations were extraordinarily exciting not only for us, but for the listeners, who valued the special combination of musical and physical performance art; through our audience, the atmosphere became more and more elated and liberating.

Today's musical world perceives and handles improvisation in a particular way. For example, jazz improvisation is based on familiar solos and runs; everyone feels and hears that this is jazz. We sought a markedly different kind of improvisation, perhaps not even improvisation. It is defined not by its musical style, but by its atmosphere, effect, and internal experience, intuition. One key element of such music creation is the contact between the musicians, the common involvement. Because our bond of friendship was strong and deep, there was no obstacle to making unusual forms of music or being on the same wavelength when performing publicly. Later we became aware of other important and defining elements.

As a result of our lived experiences, many internal images took shape that we shared with each other and tried to convey as well as possible. For me, even up to this day, a favorite such image is the view of Budapest at dawn, when I walk home over the empty Margit Bridge in the drizzling rain. It is still dark; above the Danube and the houses of Pest, the scarlet light of daybreak appears. The rain hitting my face enhances the experience, as does the large patent leather suitcase I am carrying, which I open at the middle of the bridge, releasing white doves into the air. In the silence of dawn you can hear their wings rustling. Freedom and spiritual peace fill the air on the bridge; a floating, calm plume of sound spreads through me, and the birds fly in the first rays of the rising sun.

I would have liked to express these and similar images in music, but alone I felt inadequate to the task; I needed companions. In the time that followed, I was powerfully affected by my fellow band-founders; I think this was mutual, as we became one of the most unusual underground bands of the 1980s at home and abroad.

Upward Trajectory

We paired our unusual improvisation with a powerful performance art style even at our first concerts. This meant that the music's liberating effect came with an expressive, ecstatic movement springing from spiritual encounter, radiating the limitless burst of freedom. This sort of motion had a great impact on young people, since the teenage and young adult years are often characterized by physical reticence and half-heartedness. At that moment where movement attains a state of dance charged by an internally fueled, self-expressive, internal radiance, it causes the desire for freedom to pour forth. Just how the listeners accessed this same state, we did not know at the time; we just guessed it. We felt that our internal freedom and joyous music-making were somehow being transmitted to the audience. We experienced a musical state of mind essentially new to us, the kind that liberates a person completely and creates an internal, secret world. We were capable of expressing the voyage inside it directly, without any inhibition, through music and the associated performance. The audience's reaction was amazingly positive. Our music was ecstatic, and the effects were enhanced by a spiritual encounter so powerful that it overwhelmed everything.

A boundless force pulled us. We found purpose only in doing something that no one before us had done. We wanted to approach everything creatively, without copying or imitating anything. We had no wish to join the ranks of humdrum music-manufacturers; we wished to avoid all traps and live in continual creative fever. This was true not only for our music-making, but also for our studies and internal development; all of this worked together as a tremendous driving force.

Long ago, but still today, it is a fad, even habitual, to "fabricate" bands and throw them out onto the music market. We live in a world of fashionable talent-search shows and artificially produced celebrities; we don't notice that the show is lying through and through, that it has nothing to do with the true challenges of life. It doesn't let you glimpse behind the scenes; just puppet-dolls turn up on the conveyor belt, gunked and covered with glaze, bereft of individuality and uniqueness, functioning as market products. Hoping for prosperity, fame, and glamor, they will produce money for the managers hiding in the background. The road to false success has always been like this. But there were and are those who cannot and will not melt into this mediocre world of false idol-seeking and crowd-pleasing. These are the creative young people representing an alternative path, who seek genuine and true challenges and wish to realize their own visions.

Since man is a social being, adaptability is one of our basic characteristics. A question is who and what we adapt to and on what grounds. In today's information flow, it is difficult to make correct and wise decisions. On a given topic, all sorts of data, information, documents and background literature are at our disposal. Orientation is difficult, especially when the information is "smudged" intentionally or unintentionally, making the communication as confusing as possible. However, the search for a clear and true path can be guided from within, from our soul, which helps us with intuition and perception.

During the initial years of the band, we talked extensively about what we experienced internally when making or listening to music; we tried to decode its secret and magic from every angle. We were deeply concerned with how best to reach this internal experience through our shared music-making, how to transmit it most genuinely and offer the audience a profoundly livable, shocking, true experience. We did everything to redeem the unacceptably poor outlook, music, and perspective of the average youth of those times, pointing out entirely new directions and possibilities. For all of us this was a great, defining task that affected our entire lives. In our lives, these became key elements: the striving for constant creation, a positive way of thinking together, shared noetic transformation, whose rays attracted young people our age; as a result, our wider circle of friends kept on expanding. More and more of them wanted to be with us, more and more came to our concerts, because they felt that they were receiving something from us that they did not find elsewhere. A successful concert gave rise to a spiritual purification and a sense of freedom, free of poses, that meant liberation from everyday burdens and an ordering of the soul. Unclouded freedom, the force of experiences lived out together, love, unbridled glee, and the ferocious display of the above—all of this broke through the limits erected by the system, which were already starting to sway.

Many people might wonder how fame came to a band whose music received no media publicity whatsoever, or if it did, then just disparaging and dismissive critique.

The following answers can apply even today to the question of how a band or other production can get off the treadmill.

- It was we ourselves, not others, who brought the band into being.
- The band was not advertised; rather, word spread about it.
- We proved that we could attain success even without investing money in the band.
- We did not want to follow and fit in with trends; rather, in some measure we started a new endeavor.
- We did not count among the money-worshippers; we didn't want to put out an album or play for money.
- We had no wish to perform productions and please the crowd; instead, we tried to mobilize a positive, shared spiritual energy and turn this into a shared experience.
- We were not interested in exteriors, but in the working of internal forces.

Some elements of these perspectives apply equally to the 1980s and to underground bands today. The essence is perhaps the same as for the rebellious youth of any era: they have no desire to fit into a trendy and controlled system but instead endeavor to realize their own unique world.

As a particularly important element I highlight our way of thinking, which opposed trends and artistic snobbery and did not tolerate compromise. We did not want to grab attention through externals; rather, we based our musical performances and attitudes on the effects of spiritual tremors, relying entirely on the workings of internal forces. We rehearsed in various basement clubs, factory cultural rooms, and apartment basements, where the opportunity was given. We obtained our amplifiers and basic equipment on our own. On weekends, on top of school, we worked at construction sites as assistants and thus were able to earn enough money to buy what we needed. Our rehearsals gradually took a quite interesting direction. The initial period consisted mainly of selecting and playing songs from Western music that could be considered alternative. However, even from the beginning, this was not enough for us. We first tried to play out the improvisations in the songs according to our own conceptions, and as these allowed us more and more space for our own emotional world, we devoted rehearsals to exploring them as freely as we could.

Later, when we were already trying to make only our own music, everyone came to rehearsals with musical or visual ideas based on his own thoughts and feelings. For me, a picture-based musical approach dominated. This meant that I tried to pour into musical form, with the help of the guitar strings, the experiences that had appeared in images generated by my inner intuitions. There was never any pressure or expectation regarding the authorship of the music. Some of the musical ideas were realized as a shared experience, and the main point was for everyone to enjoy himself; this way, a good atmosphere and artistic environment could come about. We usually distorted the guitar through the tube amp at the cathartic moments, thus enhancing the effect. This was how, for the first time, I felt the intuitive impact of the musical freedom and mindset of Hendrix's songs. With ever richer and freer practice, we stretched the boundaries of the improvisational parts.

Over the years we had many practice spaces. At that time it was not easy to find a place where you could make a racket and turn up the volume. There was a club called the Black Hole where our band practiced for a few years: that is, we received a small practice room that only we could use, where we kept our equipment. Above the club was the Ganz-Mávag Cultural House, where one could hold concerts for larger audiences. We gave a sold-out concert there, with the ritual theater, to an audience of three thousand. In creating the Black Hole, the club's operators intended to support, with a rehearsal space, those acts that could draw an audience. I can briefly characterize the club as dark, warm, and interesting. More and more alternative bands started to perform there, and the attendance burgeoned as well. Every representative of the alternative world showed up. We didn't want to get tied up with any trend; that is, we took our own path, and we had definite ideas about what we wanted to achieve.

In the midst of the fashion trends of the time, we wore entirely everyday clothes, which perhaps resembles today's "second-hand" trend, since as students we could not afford a fancier getup. But the infinite freedom and unity of our inner radiance was evident onstage.

With this attitude, we almost completely shut out all external interference that would have limited our conceptions. This way, we were free to dispose of our own spirituality which, gathered together, guaranteed us total freedom. The band worked as a true ensemble. There was no "frontman" in the group, propped up as a media star; each of us represented the same force. Each of us did his part with full heart and dedication, and the others accepted and trusted him. We treated each other as equals, since we were friends. Everyone had an equal voice in musical issues and in planning and carrying out productions. We expected this from each other, but not in a demanding way. Each one honored the other, and we influenced each other instinctively. Our tight friendship had an impact on a large cohort of young people at that time; everyone wanted to be a member of this community.

We realized that the nature of our music, our automatic and spontaneous speech-generation, typical of our concerts, and the content of the texts themselves, greatly resembled the shamanic music and song researched by Vilmos Diószegi. The monotonous drum rhythm that gradually became ecstatic, the content of the shamanic lyrics and articulation, the melody world had astonishing correspondences with what we had started to discover and bring about from within, entirely by instinct, with our own particular worldviews. Naturally we studied shamanic music and its practical methods, and we sought an explanation for the common traits. Éva Bányai's active waking hypnosis aroused our interest too, since the altered state of consciousness at the concerts was an active state as well, which at times could mean a trance state. Alongside my studies, I immersed myself in an investigation of brain function and the subjective perception of time, and took interest in the mechanism of the internal images occurring on the endless horizons of the plane of thought. From Zen Buddhism and other Eastern religious philosophy I also gleaned that meditation and trance states have a common basis, hypnosis. This suggestive activity worked splendidly in shamanic circles as well.

More than ten years of classical music studies had a decisive influence on me, and I tried to use them to activate our conceptions. Our first major insight was when we became aware that a simple melody or piece of music could be cathartic. Even a single musical sound can be so on its own. The effect depends on the soul and internal energy that we involve when we activate this sound. It is by no means certain that a virtuoso musician without a soul, hacking for money, can reach, with a single sound, the effect of a less skilled musician who lives out the music and makes it ring with spiritual energy, that is, with ancient transcendent knowledge. Examples of this can be found is the deep and soul-gripping performance of authentic musicians even today.

In the band's initial and golden period, ego and narcissism were the most dangerous traps lurking for us, traps we could easily have fallen into, since we consciously did not desire to become part of the dreary, average, and controlled social community. However, we felt a continual urge, with our music and mentality, to expand the spiritual and emotional world of our audience and anyone else, to liberate them from everyday drear, and, to this end, to give them something at our concerts, without fail. In this we succeeded. In the following pages I will try to circumscribe this "something" and explain its special function.

Enlightenment

The concerts' freedom and our interior free flow had a strange and entirely progressive effect on our music and the accompanying experience. Interestingly, it created an altered state, perhaps a trance state, not only in us but among our audience members. One after another of our friends and acquaintances told us that they had not experienced anything like this at concerts before. These observations applied not only to our music, but to the accompanying experiences. We did not want to take part in the entertainment industry or be victimized by it. We rebelled against the artificial, mechanical, life-alienating, soul-trampling fabrication of industry products. The internal forces we were experiencing clearly signaled the direction we needed to follow. We saw that a human soul cannot be a product, our internal feelings could not be bought and sold like potatoes. Similarly, a cathartic experience or spiritual encounter offered by a suggestive performance cannot be marketed.

It is important to recognize that we are not capable of perceiving all of the countless influences coming from the outside world. We don't perceive ultrasound, for instance, which bats use superbly to find their way in the dark, or, in the case of light, ultraviolet rays. That is, our perceptions have biological boundaries. These stimulus thresholds can change depending on how tired we are, what mood we are in, our interest. As a result, the perception of a given stimulus can differ for each person. During the process of perception, we apprehend stimuli with the help of receptors and sensor cells on the surface of the cell membranes. Every receptor and sensory organ has an adequate stimulus appropriate to it. From the receptors, the stimulus is transported by sensory nerve pathways to the corresponding areas of the nervous system, where these are converted. Here we arrive at brain function, which the following pages will discuss. Because of our perceptive limitations, we cannot name the kind of stimulus perceptions that touch our soul or psyche. What makes something or someone appealing to us? What stimulus effect causes us to be in love with a particular person, or what gives us the chills when we see or hear a work of art? In certain situations, we get embarrassed and our hands start to sweat.

It seems that the purpose of our sensory organs, as defined here, is not to acquaint us with the outside world to its original and full extent, but simply to transmit as much to us as we need to stay alive. They serve the practical needs of our everyday life and help us with our practical lifestyle. Yet this reinforces the possibility that it is not the acuity of our known and defined sensory organs that determines the depth of our world knowledge or our closeness to reality, but rather the force of the psyche, which makes use of them. With the help of our sensory organs and noetic forces, we can indeed arrive at a fuller knowledge of the world and life. We can temporarily free ourselves from our sensual and material limits, thus changing our state of consciousness. This happens to us involuntarily, for instance in our dreams, or in a hypnotic or trance state. These prove that there is perception higher than the senses.

In great discoveries and inventions, imagination and intuition play at least as great a role as sensory observations and knowledge acquired through intellect. Interestingly, things that happen in this way are classified as coincidences in today's world. Yet everything is rooted in reality. We can only approach this reality; in truth we can never decipher it. How close we come is determined by the brain's processing of perception and imagination. The more effectively we use our senses and, along with them, our imagination, the closer we come to knowing reality with the help of intuitions received from within. It is essential for us to understand that we know our consciousness only consciously, that is, not in its entirety, in its true nature. Human reception can be made universal, it can be approximated more precisely, yet the consciousness controls implanted in us constantly prevent us from grasping the totality.

My bandmate-friends and I regularly walked around the city and often tried to transmit suggestions to people walking ahead of us (primarily young women). We tried to do this by imagining the individual moving along in front of us turning her head and looking at us. We tried this quite often and found it exciting and entertaining.

In the 1980s, several trends characterized the scarce entertainment possibilities for young people. One defining trend was the alternative and underground option, which included then-extant punk and other experimental music and productions. Other trends were rock music and disco, which officially received more space and opportunities. Within rock music, however, there were certain restrictions and limits, even then. Disco, on the other hand, received a wide platform and grew into a booming business. In a way that surprised me, university clubs took this up and offered it opportunities as well. There were hardly any clubs where young people open to something new could meet. As a result, the house party was one of the typical forms of entertainment of the time. Word would spread from mouth to mouth about good house parties, in a time when the supply of landline phones was limited. In Budapest, the Ádám pub on today's Andrássy street and the Erzsébet pub on Nagykörút were the key places where young people met.

Besides the more interesting programs scheduled by university clubs, there was yet another interesting place we frequented. This was the Young Artists Club (FMK), visited by young people representing many alternative artistic tendencies. Mainly art students and older alternative artists went there, but self-taught creators showed up as well. Of course there were staff there for internal security, but you could enter with a personal ID, and the permanent members could freely bring in a guest. The alternative and underground community of the capital met at that place. Interestingly, here you did not find those bands and artists that had received an official forum: those that the system held on a leash, who received a censored form of opportunity in the media and at public events. There was a constant crowd at the club; you could barely get inside. Nonetheless, we had to be careful in our assessment of the company there and in our own communications, since we would inevitably encounter fake artists and snobs who showed up just to be trendy and show off, and who put up an "alternative lifestyle" front, perhaps while performing internal security duties. They lacked true and natural spiritual freedom, openness, and a sincere ownership of their individuality. Yet these false signals did not break through the walls of our souls, since our company of friends communicated through internal channels that could not be tapped. Of course there were still people who could make things difficult for the alternative and underground world.

After our concerts we often made our way to the Ferde pub at the Buda bridgehead of the Margit Bridge, one of the pubs in Budapest that stayed open after midnight, where you could receive a tasty bean soup at night in addition to beer.

In music we were practically omnivores. We were continually receiving music from each other and from our circle of friends; on our own we followed and curated the musical tendencies important to us. We were most interested in unusual and preferably experimental music. In the midst of limited opportunities, we often recorded interesting songs from the radio, which came to us from some distant, crackling station. We then evaluated these together and tried to live them out emotionally. We were interested not in copying their melodies but rather in determining what kind of effect they could have and why. At our parties we kept on introducing each other to newer and newer songs and analyzing them to their depths, touching on every detail, step by step, playing a hundred times the parts that stood out for us. This process made our activities quite interesting within our circle, and the common spiritual vibrations attracted our wider expanse of friends as well.

We usually listened to the music important to us at a very high volume. We carried each other along the emotional currents of our imaginations; if necessary, we bawled, if necessary, we screamed or laughed our heads off.

This caused all sorts of people to seek out our company; they continually wanted to party with us.

At the musical parties where we showed up, we always danced in an unusual way—of course, just to the ecstatic songs that we had brought along with us, insisting that these be listened to, because that way we could truly revel. We moved to these songs with such vehemence that everyone just stood and shook their heads in amazement; later, when they felt that the frenzied hell of freedom had been unleashed, they too, interestingly, started to move without restraint. I would describe this unusual dance as the opposite of the stereotypical dances of the time. We gave room to motions motivated by complete and boundless freedom; we let this do its work. If necessary, we quivered on the floor, or twitching and jumping, we followed the music's rhythm and magic, sinking into its effect. This was in no way an affected and snobbish routine, but rather a sincere manifestation fueled from within and coming from our hearts and souls, performed with full involvement, almost instinctively. Thinking it over, we can grasp that ecstatic movement, and not a wobbly waddle, goes well with ecstatic songs. This requires an internal, cathartic freedom, which makes the unraveling possible.

These shared music listenings, parties, emotional charges, and spiritual immersions fueled the soul-stirring and shocking parts of our concerts. We always brought something new and unexpected to our rehearsals, then tried to glean an internal charge from it, which gave all of us further inspiration. We built, step by step, from such experiences, and tried to enhance the effect triggered by the atmosphere. At concerts we had to accomplish this on the spot. This resembled the kind of sensual deception that has the positive effect of bringing something real to life. When at first my legs started to shake, and I felt a warm flash in my chest from the emotional and spiritual charge radiated by the room full of listeners, this signaled for me the presence and working of an invisible, as yet unfamiliar force. It was similar to when we listen to deep, good music or watch a cathartic performance, except that here the effects came much more strongly and intensely, with wider dimensions. The unbridled magic of the emotional and spiritual trance state born of shared involvement nearly swept away the internal barriers of anxiety and half-heartedness, and a rough, whirling communal joy took their place. Desires nearly came to life, and the waves of emotion became palpable in the presence of something ethereal, where the music and beat zigzagged in people's chests as a carrier material.

Before proceeding, I would like to give a brief overview of art as I have come to understand it over the years. Many have tried and continue to try to define art, which in fact is no simple task. I, too, will make an attempt based on what I lived through and experienced over the course of my musical career.

The Creative Force of Archaic Transcendent Knowledge as a Hidden Source of Art and Science

For me, art is an activity that can make an impact inside a person.

Art is generally defined as the expression or application of human creative skill and imagination. Through these, creations emerge that are valued primarily for their beauty or emotional power. For me, however, such a definition fails to explain how the effect can come about. The answer may lie in the special relation between our brain function and internal life, which can produce an effect in our soul. There is intuition: an inborn, instinctive sense fulfillable as active, magical knowledge, magical because it can help us recognize the deeper common properties and features of our seemingly disparate experiences. More vividly, more conspicuously, and through different means, we can experience the original, hidden content of an image or idea that reached us through a purely rational route. Alongside the senses, direct intuitive cognition takes us closer to the essence of things and in the best of circumstances can represent the upper limit of knowledge. We might call this enlightenment, which assists spiritual cognition. Its realization can come about through spiritual encounter and internal picturing, coupled with internal experience. We can also call this the initiation of the soul. Such a spiritual encounter can truly work when the initiation and involvement occur as deeply as possible for the sake of the goal at hand. The road to such initiation of the soul can assist sacral cognition as a contemporary form of transfiguration. The result of this process is faith in something, namely, that which we live out and do. This series of steps leads to true art or rewarding scientific activity, which we can also call transcendent ancient knowledge. The essential point is that this chain of processes instigated by our brain's transmission has creative power.

In the figure on the next page, I would like to represent the working mechanism of archaic transcendent knowledge. I call it transcendent knowledge because its application evokes and strengthens each person's natural capacity to exert a palpable noetic, emotional, and spiritual effect on another.

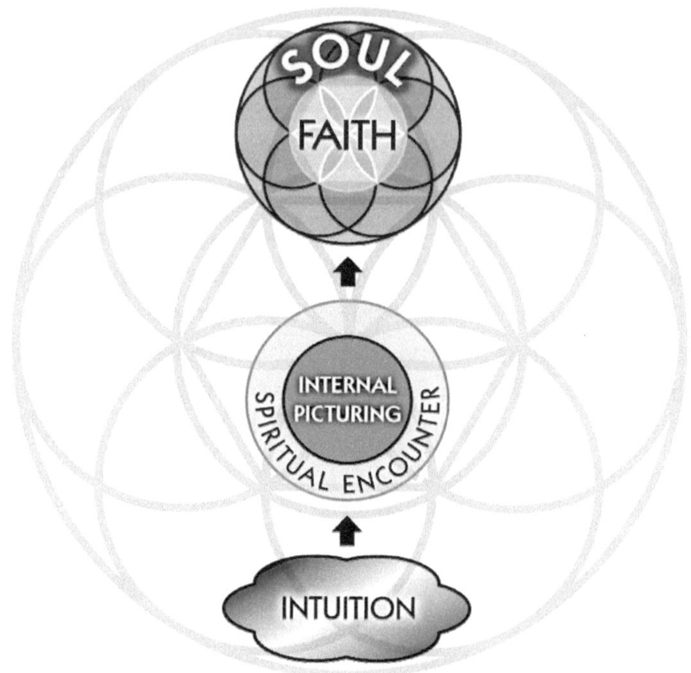

The end of the process appears in the energy field represented by the soul, which I identify here with the ancient symbol of the Seed of Life. This is most important folk symbol of the sun, a basic element of the Flower of Life emblem and a sacred symbol.

This symbol can be found almost all over the world, in countless cultures, signifying a world of pure forms and proportions. I chose it because we can adopt it as a metaphor depicting the interrelation of the universe's psyche and all life.

The realization of the intuition through spiritual encounter is assisted by internal picturing (imagination). The stronger our internal picturing, the more effective our faith in what we do. This strong faith, mobilized by the soul, radiates outward to everyone, independent of space or time. We call that an effect. It is the essence and foundation stone of artistic and scientific creation.

The center of the process is spiritual encounter realized through internal picturing, which actually signifies a kind of transformation that affects the soul through the feelings. This is an innate capacity, since in our childhood, when we played with toys or listened to stories, we lived it out spiritually, by instinct.

The emergent internal experience affects the function of the soul through the radiation of faith; as a result, it can be transmitted from one human to another without words, and can exert an effect as a manifestation outside of space and time.

Our faith represents the energy path that the ancients knew. In their world, faith was the bridge connecting the present with the future. They believed that they could reach their gods by crossing bridges of copper, silver, and gold. Only pure and blameless people could make their way across these glistening bridges of light. This world, independent of time and space, could be reached only on the wings of the soul, with projected consciousness, entrancement, and magic steeds.

The soul appears as a link between the body and the psyche. For instance, the world of the imagination, fantasy, lies on the soul's terrain. The soul as a mirror of our feelings can be rambling, unruly, the source of eruptive joy and pain, love and hate: that is, archaic spiritual manifestations that still characterize us all. Dream and daydreaming can be included here too. The human psyche assists pure thought, free of pictures, based on learned knowledge, and helps us navigate the matters of the world. This is how creation, arising from the recesses of the soul and formed by our psyche, can become truly potent and real. The soul is that invisible carrying force capable of bringing the effect from person to person and, in certain cases, influencing crowds. Consider feelings, for instance, which can affect and be transmitted to a person or people in an invisible form.

This carrying force can be mobilized by the process of transcendent, enchanting knowledge introduced in the preceding pages.

This magical knowledge offers the possibility of real and complete personal power. This power allows us to hold our fate in our hands and helps us acquire those experiences that fulfill our personal lives. There is no doubt that the most harmful idol of today's world, money, gives people more free space virtually, but since it is just one of the arsenals of power exercised over a particular system, it falls far short of the fate-altering forces provided by personal power. The possession of personal power incorporates such important elements as spiritual function, spirituality, love, and emotional reciprocity.

In today's world, we hide behind virtuality. Repressing feelings has nearly become a fad; we rush past each other numbly. As they grow up, children experience and learn that the sincere expression of feelings is unacceptable. They suppress their feelings, try to fine-tune them, and thus erase what they live out internally. As a result, their personal relationships fail. Roots in true depth are lost; people lose the capacity to open up to others, since they do not understand what feeling and spiritual function are. So let us give room to our feelings, leave our inhibitions behind, and experience our personal power.

Susceptibility to hypnosis is interrelated with the liveliness of the imagination, the richness of its combinations, the capacity for profound spiritual encounter, a synthesizing mode of thought, and the ability to change states of consciousness frequently and flexibly, i.e., with spiritual sensitivity. It is also important to develop the capacity to switch quickly and easily between the brain's hemispheres. These are the key elements of ancient transcendent knowledge.

Developing the usage and working of the right brain is an effective route to optimal relative brain function. Clearly each person has a different ratio of right and left brain usage. Unfortunately, people are generally unaware of how the function of the two hemispheres affects their actions and lives, or that the ratio can be changed, altering their internal life and spiritual function. We should remember that the ratio of brain hemisphere utilization can be developed: namely, we can possibly achieve its operation through conscious practice. Far Eastern gurus, hermits, fakirs, and monks have this capacity and apply it at different levels.

To sum up again: the left and right brain hemispheres basically use two divergent working mechanisms. The left hemisphere is responsible for thought that follows and applies an analytical, didactic, verbal, and logical sequence; the right hemisphere, for artistic, visual, and perceptive activities. These include intuition, internal picturing and spiritual encounter, which are the basis for the application of soul-moving, archaic transcendental knowledge. It is perhaps an oversimplification to say that the left hemisphere is responsible for the detailed comprehension of a given thing; the right hemisphere, for the big picture. Both the left and right hemispheres are capable of perception at a high level; although they differ from each other, they participate in our thought, inferences, and intricate spiritual processes.

To use our brain function effectively, it is especially important that we be able to employ both brain hemispheres at the necessary level. Thus it is essential that we bring into balance the forces that form our two attitudes: the intellectual and the spiritual, which we hold inside us and which are influenced by our brain function.

The intellectual attitude treats the known world as an object, analyzing, examining it in detail with systematic procedures. Someone moving on the purely and exclusively intellectual plane, devoid of emotion, ignoring and displacing the spiritual function, wants to take possession of the known world, to mine and exploit every single one of its givens, even if he knows that he can harm his future with this.

The other kind of person, the one with a spiritual and noetic attitude, tries to act in unity with the world, seeking not to subjugate it, but rather to help it work by being at its service, thus strengthening harmony. Such a person does not perceive the world as a reality confined within limits, defined according to human laws and precepts, but rather as a space that makes room for the noetic encounter with the infinite and the experience of transformed space and time. Emotional openness combines with an internal sense of freedom radiating positive energy. To attain this, it is indispensable to live out and experience social relationships in a genuine, natural way. Thus we can feel the other person's vibrations and can interpret a flash of the eye.

Our internal picturing and imagination can evoke wonders. They allow us not only to access and draw on what we have already lived and experienced, but sometimes to encounter things that no one has lived or experienced before. The feeling resembles that which we experience when we step out of our familiar room for the first time into the whirl of an unknown world, opening the possibility of unfamiliar experiences and new ideas and paths. Such is the Einsteinian space-time paradox, which is based on intuition entirely at odds with everyday experience, and which probably never would have been formulated if our perception and attendant knowledge had been the only tools at hand. It is no coincidence that Einstein deemed imagination much more important than knowledge, since the imagination's storehouse is infinite.

Let us assume that our everyday thought can be called finite, since we are limited by our extant experience and knowledge set. In contrast, the imagination allows us to reach beyond our limits, beyond our finite knowledge and practical skills. Internal picturing and the imagination are an unconscious part of our mind. Our internal picturing arises from our memories and acquired knowledge, among other things, and combines these in a new, unique way. If we are unable to recall something consciously, the stored code to this is still in our imagination.

Our imagination and internal picturing can help us access even those things that we have largely ignored. This can include someone's behavior, a background detail, a tiny facial movement, a piece of music or a detail in it. It follows that our internal picturing and imagination belong to those parts of the brain excluded from our conscious thought. That, among other reasons, is why we unconsciously carry the spiritual burdens of our parents, grandparents, and ancestors: our upbringing and relationships with our parents and relatives, their spiritual effects, are encoded in us without our doing.

One feature of our internal picturing capacity is that, drawing on our infinite storehouse, it assigns numerous patterns to things we have experienced or learned; it is the key to our problem-solving capacity, that is, creativity. Many scientists and inventors, by giving space to their imagination and internal picturing, have experienced breakthroughs with previously unsolved problems.

Consequently, for true, nonmechanical art and all other creative activities, internal picturing is the seed. Given this, it is not surprising to hear artists and scientists say that an idea or conception that speaks to the world was simply born in their heads. It seems that during internal picturing, our brains bring things into being or solve problems, and when they finish, they hand them over to our conscious mind, so that our left hemispheres can process them further. It seems that true creative force is activated while the brain's right hemisphere is at work.

Our internal picturing, our imagination, is capable of working in the background and exerting an effect while our conscious brain, using the left hemisphere, handles our daily problems. We do not have to exert our will to attain a goal; we need only believe that we can bring our visions to fruition. While we solve problems of everyday life, we think non-visually with the help of information processed from received stimuli and our perceptions. At such times, we have no other option and support than logical thinking, which always limits our knowledge and acquired skills to some degree, according to its measure. In some cases, it can lead us astray; often it is incapable of solutions. At such times we try to solve the problem before us with our left hemisphere, which makes use of poor mechanistic algorithms that a computer could solve more effectively and quickly. Of course, at a certain point our thought supported by internal picturing needs to make use of reason and logic, but first we should let our right hemisphere do its work, letting our psyche draw on on our soul. We can be truly effective if we create a balance between the functions of the left and right hemispheres.

A human is basically a visual being: the dominant part of our brain is dedicated to visual processing. In our everyday lives we continually process visual information in pictorial form; thus, our brains are especially strong in this area. It comes as no surprise that internal picturing is at the center of ancient transcendent knowledge.

The capacity for internal picturing is nothing other than seeing those pictures that we create with "spiritual eyes." This is the truly effective mode of both creative and problem-solving thought. The soul's infinite storehouse provides an excellent basis for our noetic function. However, for this to work, it is indispensable that we set the soul in motion and experience its magic. The soul's operative motor is the heart. Our hearts not only keep our bodies alive, pumping blood into our veins, but also set our souls in motion. Namely, when we feel with our hearts, we become capable of seeing with our souls. The balance of the soul's and heart's functions can fulfill our lives and fill us with joy and love. However, we need to develop the momentum of this balanced communication within ourselves. This comes about through love. This is why we feel joy over a creative process that we have brought forth; we love to do it, and it fills us with love. In the process of magical, transcendent knowledge, hidden creative power induces admiration. Whoever is in awe of his subject, or brings something into the world in which he has participated deeply—that is, whoever is transformed by what he does—takes part in the magical process.

A creation becomes lasting, that is, it leaves a mark on people, if it can exert an effect. It is possible to exert an effect with the application of the process described in the preceding pages, so that its final impact mobilizes our spiritual function. The soul is our special, dimensionless energy source manifested as energy outside of space and time. It works independently of space, time, and distance, it has no past or future, yet at the same time it is capable of accessing those regions that the consciousness can neither reach nor grasp. The soul is a storehouse of knowledge that our consciousness might deem inaccessible, even unfathomable. Another important property of the soul is that as an energy carrier, with proper internal direction, it can be transmitted to another person, other people. One universally verifiable property of this energy source is that it can change physical matter; that is, when our noetic activity is altered under the influence of our spiritual function, the workings of our heart, biochemical processes, and other organs also change.

Openness, Love: A Positive Force

Very few are familiar with the ancient force that works through love manifested in openness. People today are languishing from lack of love. If we turn to another person with such openness that the spark of love glows forth, then the other person will feel this, and from then on, the two can communicate on a different plane entirely.

The absence of either one of these factors will radiate negative energy. If a person is very open, for instance, raising children in a family that operates on modern principles, but puts little energy into showing love, this does not carry positive energy. Nor will it do so if love rules in the family or in human relationships, but openness and sincerity are missing or impaired. So the basic requirement for positive energy is the unity of openness and love, their balance, and their sustenance. Love is positive energy emerging from the soul.

In the band, our strong friendships, arising from real-life contact, undergirded our ongoing music creation and its processes. This gave rise to sincere openness toward each other, as well as love and enthusiasm for each other as people. This is the basis of any fruitful human relationship. For us, the resulting positive forces, working together, created strong relational energy. It is important to remember that only through personal contact can love and openness be realized effectively and positive energy be created.

In such a positive spiritual force field, it is easy to bring intuition to life. The shared experience of spiritual encounter and internal picturing has such a strong effect on the circle of participants that it multiplies their faith in the production, the creation. A musical, other artistic, or scientific creation arising in this manner becomes suggestive because faith, induced by ancient transcendent, magical knowledge (explained in the previous pages) radiates outward to the participants.

We need only consider common prayer, when people on different continents, in different places, pray at the same time for the sake of something in particular, according to old tradition. A shared thought strives for realization. It is no accident that this sort of common prayer and its role in human life have survived up to this day. Common prayers affect us through the power of the psyche; it was no accident that our ancestors left us this tradition. In churches, the same gospels are read; in wars and catastrophes, the call to simultaneous prayer is intentional, as it has an enormous effect. Rituals of the ancient world were likewise carried out communally, and the members of the tribe experienced the prayers together, prayers for healing or other goals. Some Far-Eastern fakir stunts work on the same principle. For example, during a levitation performance, the viewers experience something that seems real but is in fact a virtual impression, an illusion; that is, during the stunt, the fakir is sitting in one place. The key here is the formation of a spiritual force field among the viewers, as well as the powerful experience of an image formed by internal intuition, which conveys strong faith to the audience as well. This results in a profoundly lived internal experience that seems true. If a photographer or video-maker (an outsider to the stunt) recorded it, then those viewing the pictures would see, to their surprise, a fakir sitting in one place and people staring at him. The interesting thing here is that the energy transmits itself and works without words.

Today there are fewer and fewer theatrical performances in which truly great actors perform the kind of soul-instructing work whose effect brings the viewers to tears. In today's virtual world, the tendency is to relegate creation proceeding from transcendent knowledge entirely to the background. Perhaps in the realm of classical music concerts, there are still performances with such depth and cathartic effect.

Returning to the band: we sought the kind of intuition that could be the source of this process. Clearly we could not turn to a world of pre-written repertory music but had to set off on an untraveled path.

The world of sounds is inexhaustible; that is, it can stimulate our mood and thought in all sorts of ways. For instance, a sound that conveys the intuition can be a beat or a melody. If we let it do its own work, it can be experienced in itself; that is, it works an effect inside us. If we wish to convey this experience, we can do so in pictures, in which dreamlike, unreal images may play a part. This is how song lyrics can be born. Our language is a particular device that projects these images brilliantly. Our soul receives this internal picturing, we profoundly feel the magic revealed in it, to the point where we start to have faith in it. This can also work its effect without words. The images evoked through internal picturing, combined with spiritual encounter and faith, sustain the process. This is an unstable, sensitive state that must be honored and protected from harsh external interruptions.

What we started to do, we couldn't name at first; later we called it flow-music or life-music. It wasn't just some kind of improvisation, but the result of the process previously described. This initiation of the soul evoked in us an infinite sense of freedom, a kind of purification.

Our first decisive concert where we were able to convey this successfully to the audience was an event organized by the KKS (Budapest University of Economics Experimental Studio). That same week, at a concert organized by the Castle Club, the resulting experience was what I consider music creation generated by soul-motivating magic. When we appeared before the listeners with this elementally powerful production—which was so new that all on its own, it burst everything open, kicked everything up—it paralyzed and liberated people at the same time.

But where did this music creation get its elemental force? Perhaps the answer is we sought the spark of intuition in instinctively elemental, ancient images. We tried to express them through sound, transforming them in the visual dimension, and to convey the manifest, activated image stream through our shared music creation. For this we needed a certain bravery, since this approach broke with everything that people were used to so far. It seemed that a kind of openness and empathetic capacity was needed for the initial spark only; the rest came almost automatically, since the continual internal picturing sustained the process. I didn't know what was happening inside the other band members, but I felt that whatever I did that was good for me, was also good for them, good, in fact, because it had a tremendous effect. After the concerts, when we talked about our experiences, it also became clear that the images we had experienced were almost identical. In subsequent concerts we built three or four segments into an hour's worth of material, each one conveying images we had captured in advance: for instance, the experience of falling down a waterfall or rapids, or standing on a cliff in a storm and looking around at the sky split by lightning. These images we had already internalized; during the concert, we glided from one image to the next, living out the experience that we tried to express and convey with music. The empathetic force field came into being at concerts thanks to the working of the brain's mirror neurons and effect mechanism, which I will discuss in the following chapter.

The appropriate application of the above principles by the musicians and audience can endow a person with such force that he can act on patterns that have not been established in advance and can express things that seem special to others. Perhaps this is how the first (and one of the most important) phases of the band's work began: that is, we realized that our music-making could not entail writing songs in advance; instead, the production would be born in front of the audience. We tried with such imaginative force to perform the elements of images that we had preconceived in detail, that these had an impact on the other band members and strengthened the total effect. In addition, this shared imaginative force could reach a point where the audience saw what we were living out. It is no surprise that many sound recordings of the old concerts have remained, and not all the musical material really came out that well; but for the audience, that was not the only carrying force or enthralling element, as it was accompanied by the transmission of our internal images, and its frenetic effect. This was further enabled by our performance-art style, as well as our automatic lyric generation, which brought us into contact with shaman music research.

When, at an interview, I was asked what I would say about releasing an album of our music, I answered that I didn't want an album at all. Perhaps this can be understood in terms of the preceding discussion and the aforementioned levitation stunts, since this experience, which seemed real and was lived profoundly, cannot be played back on an electronic data storage device. The transmission to the audience of the spiritual encounter taking place in our souls during concerts, along with our faith, works there, at that location; none of it can be discerned from a photograph or video. This also raises an interesting question: why the band's activity had such a strong effect on Western youth of the 1980s. At concerts abroad, the lyrics were in Hungarian, the singer sang in Hungarian—this went without saying, since we are Hungarian—and we believed and were aware that the magic would do its work anyway. At the end of our first concert abroad, the crowd stood in silence, as if some mysterious positive force had torn across the room. They probably had never experienced anything like this.

Besides creating musical performance art, we were dedicated to conveying internal experiences that we lived out in organic unity with the music. This meant that we always tried to convey to the audience a positive radiancy, which allowed mass suggestion to occur. This could only work when it had to do with things that were true to us, believable, and livable; for us too, existing in that process was an experience and a pleasure. The most beautiful example of the manifestation of positive force is the mother rocking her child, when she hums her little one to sleep, radiating love. In this intimate state, the child and mother are under hypnosis; such suggestion, accompanied by singing and rocking, is the most beautiful and natural hypnosis given to us by life, a hypnosis that involves an effect by one person on another. In this altered state of consciousness, a sensitive love relationship comes about, which strengthens the trust and relationship between the mother and child.

This sort of positive force must be mobilized in some way during any kind of artistic activity. During the production one must create and internalize mutual acceptance, which must be based on trust. At the concerts, the first important dreamlike images, formed with musical sounds, assured this state. This was the beginning of a journey where, regardless of the situation, only positive energies were at work: that is, we lived out shared experiences, strengthened our inner selves, released our tensions and worries, and lived with complete inner freedom.

This experience resembles that which we have in our youth when we form true and lasting friendships with a few who merit it. At first a given person just seems sympathetic to us; then, steadily, mutual trust and acceptance come into being. Common goals take the relationship forward and deepen the hypnosis. Let us also consider how romantic love takes shape, its force sweeping everything away. This kind of positive force exists and works in our genes.

The musical journey at the concerts led us inevitably into a trance state where the cerebral hemispheres' increased functional efficiency allowed us to order the relationship between our body and our environment, since we had freed our tunnel vision and thus could see more clearly. It is no surprise that internal images appeared inside us such as the world, totality, the Sun, the Earth, life and death, love and hate. These primal feelings in us, as bearers of universal primal laws, unknowingly engage our subconscious, and we begin to think with our heart and soul, which can also help to cleanse our conscience.

In retrospect, I think that at our successful concerts we were able to radiate a working positive force from the stage, a far-reaching creative process capable of endowing the audience with positive energy that allows us to contend bravely with unknown challenges. The struggle with the unknown happened at two levels. The first level was the creation and sustenance of music flow; the second, the radiation of the relationship between nature and man, affecting the first level and influenced by natural effects. This level can be considered infinite, both in its cognizance and in its relation. The plunge into this infinite, unfamiliar world can be considered one of the highest creative processes. In science the situation is similar; here too, the most far-reaching discoveries are made when a person dares to step into the infinite realm of the unknown, and finds within it new roads and possibilities. Naturally this does not mean that we should erase conscious and learned things from our brains and refrain from using them, as these will also contribute to the successful creative process, even without drawing attention to their contribution. Any kind of creative process is a risk associated with strong imaginative capacity and vitality, where to arrive at a new discovery, we must turn away from the customary path, step out of our everyday rut, dive into the mysterious, and identify with the given situation or problem. It is risky because it feels frightening to set aside notions that have been deduced through proven logical methods and built up with conscious techniques. A thought born in this manner harbors a force that can change matter or bring it into being; moreover, it can destroy life, which is otherwise completely impossible from a materialistic point of view. We must understand that the psyche builds the body; our thoughts are capable of stimulating energies and thus influencing the material. Our noetic energies, with the assistance of our soul, can become transmissible to our human companions. This transmitted energy radiates internal joy, which triggers pleasure, love, and a kind of positive force in the circle of participants. Naturally, for this to happen, the energy must be conveyed; therefore, the suggestions transmitted through the production must work.

Things born in this manner have the following significance: from nothing, that is, 0, they raise something to 1. Since we can progress from 1 to 5 through conscious logical construction, the latter holds less significance, since it just involves multiplying by 5. In contrast, 1 is infinite in relation to 0; therefore, the thing created from nothing through transcendent magical knowledge has enormous meaning.

Free, Suggestive Music-Creation
Using Archaic Transcendent Knowledge

More and more clearly, we saw and felt the direction that we had almost automatically stumbled on at first. For the band to work, we needed more members, but finding the right people was no simple matter. Many could not overcome their inhibitions, or were incapable of approaching and bringing out those internal images that flashed during music creation, or were not able to give themselves over to the shared experience, the shared journey, that came to life during our cathartic music-making. There were three guys besides the founding members who could contribute outstandingly to our shared endeavors. The term "charismatic personality" might characterize the blue-eyed, blond fellow with the chiseled face, who, when he stepped into a crowded place, had all eyes glued to him. He became the bassist. Besides him, two younger guys were immediately able to process the experiences and become part of the liberated music. Both had already played in punk as well as alternative underground bands. One was a guy with psychic powers, blessed with a gift for inner transformation, which he could express with his solo guitar. The other combined fiery savagery with intelligence; even at a young age, he was suggestive, in superb command of his internal workings, and blessed with a fine sense of music. He became the kettle drummer; someone with similar qualities replaced him later on. The band changed over time and new members appeared, but this lineup characterized the defining period.

At rehearsals and concerts, an overwhelming, unstoppable and awe-inspiring force radiated from the band. We spent all our free time together; an ongoing, deep friendship nourished our soul connections. We discussed all our music-related experiences in images. We regularly reported to each other our internal experiences. Each time we listened to a new song, we shared our experiences with each other, and after listening to them many times, we analyzed the best songs' effect mechanisms. The band members shared a great passion for music collection. We sampled from a wide spectrum, except for disco, hits, and pop.

Our regular rehearsals and our lives together as friends created a force field among us and our friends, giving our path an upward trajectory. An undefinable force pulled us. Our equal involvement in all of the band's matters, achieved without any forcing, was indispensable in this regard.

We considered it worthwhile to do only those things that opened up absolutely new paths before us, through which we could live out new challenges. We wanted to approach everything creatively. We didn't want to copy things that had been produced and created by others. Thinking together continually, we worked out the structure of our next concerts and our new approaches. The goal was always to accomplish a brand new musical performance that drew on the atmosphere of a given evening. Alongside our shared creative process, there was yet another serious binding material: friendship. This was a natural force, drawing on the depths of the soul, that made the trajectory of our shared music-making almost unbreakable. Without this, the entire process would have failed. This limitless friendship released the brakes in our spiritual locomotives, the engine started to tear along, and terrific energies were released.

The band was able to work out and realize a creative process capable of creating and transmitting incredibly positive energies. The experience was enhanced by its generosity, its way of conveying the joy of inner world perception and enormous spiritual freedom. Those who received this will have an eternal memory.

From the start we had already started finding ourselves in a strange ecstatic state while making music. This resulted in a special, boundless sense of freedom and a joyous, intoxicated state of consciousness. We also found through experience that it had a transcendent effect: that is, it was something that we could transfer to each other, much like the way a yawn catches on. This ecstatic state transferred more and more to the audience as well. The working mechanisms already have explanations.

According to brain researchers, when we live an event profoundly, so-called mirror neurons are activated in our brain. These nerve cells are activated in a person's brain when he or she watches someone else's behavior, as well as when someone imitates another. Thus mirror neurons were active when we played music in an ecstatic state, as well as when someone in the audience took part in this music performance. At first it was the band members who felt and shared this effect; later it was transferred to the audience as well. These neurons ensure that we are able to empathize with others' feelings and live out their experiences even when not paying direct attention to them.

An important characteristic of the strong empathetic force field emerging at the concerts was that everyone became part of a shared world, which imperceptibly brought us all closer together. This effect manifests itself without words; everyone, moving together, experiences the force field and smiles. We suddenly feel that everyone is with us; it is as if we had always known each other. At such times it seems that we see and feel each other's souls. I believe that this will make complete sense to those readers who have already had such an experience; however, whoever has not yet experienced it will have a hard time being convinced, since today's science has not yet reached the point of explaining these effect mechanisms on the basis of verifiable definitions and laws.

The music stream generated by the internal picturing process during the band's production spread out over this force field, taking on a form that could be felt and experienced by all. From then onward, a shared faith took shape: faith in the freedom of the soul and the experience of pure, personal power, motivated by the band's suggestive, magical music-creation.

During the band's golden era, our concerts differed substantially from each other; that is, there were no two identical musical productions. We prepared for each performance separately; we always imagined a different structure, which we tried to convey to each other in advance, in pictures. We established the main junctions of the music flow in advance and entrusted each other with the implementation, but in such a way that each of us trusted the other precisely and rock-solidly; that is, this unknown did not cause any uncertainty or raise any barriers in us.

Once we mounted the stage, an interesting atmosphere resonated in the air. The first note was not in my head yet, since there was no need for it; it was not that note that dictated what followed, but rather the reverse: the first effect that arrived from the audience defined the first note. Everyone who came to our concerts watched that day's production with great anticipation, since they likewise had no idea what would happen but were sure that we were taking every possible measure to produce something that had never occurred before and would not be repeated. This was a great challenge, not only for us, but for the audience too, since everyone felt serious interdependence and the magic of anticipation glowing in the air. This excited an immense experience of freedom, which was nevertheless unfamiliar, since in contrast with the constraints of an ordinary concert in which a ready-made repertoire is performed, this musical performance contained no limiting factors.

The beginning of the concert was the magic of the moment, the desire to initiate a common experience; this radiated from the eyes and the spiritual force field of the room. The feeling was as when you are taken blindfolded into a completely dark room, and you have to decide whether anyone is in there or not. Clearly at such times those special internal "scanning organs" come into play, which do not work in everyday situations, since there is no need for them. Somehow, in the dark we can feel the soundless crowd standing around us. We needed a spark of this special intuition and revelation. For me, this suggestive magic at the beginning of the concert provided the intuition for the first sound.

To live and expand this moment in its full depth, we had to process the common spiritual vibrations, turning them into an inner experience. Following the first note and beat, the flow of sound, music, and singing was propelled by the magic of this shared experience, reinforced and experienced through internal picturing; this shaped the music of the entire concert. This process led us into a special trance state, that is, an altered state of consciousness where not only the music but also the lyrics were born automatically. It is no accident that we started to study ancient shaman music and analyze the lyrics, since we sensed that the spiritual encounters at our concerts closely resembled the kind of active waking hypnosis that the shamans incited. This is why, along with others, we called our music during this period "life music": it came into being and broke forth as a living stream, similar to our lives, where we can dictate the events of the next moment only up to a point, as we do not see ahead precisely and do not know what will happen.

The internal event of total freedom was certainly transmitted to the audience, together with the movement, murmur, and visual representation of natural forces. The music was born like a dewdrop on a wavering blade of grass in a field at dawn.

The most successful manifestation of this feeling and experience was at the Castle Club in Budapest. That club, located on today's Holy

Trinity Square, next to the Matthias Church, provided a space for those bands that drew larger crowds, even in the 1980s. At that concert we introduced a substantially new and exciting intuitive technique. On the one hand, it was here that we started to to play back, at a different speed, sounds recorded with a condenser microphone, which produced an unusual floating sound; on the other hand, we played back the entire concert in real time with the same technique, with barely perceptible delay. This technique produced a quite interesting sound-drift, entirely different from the traditional delay or echo effects of that time. The guitar sound was expansive; the entire room swam in the sounds that filled up the space. The effect was further intensified by the fact that the microphone picked up the crowd's applause and cheers along with the sounds produced by the amplifiers, and the system transmitted these sounds, with delay, back out to the audience. At this concert we also experimented with a wind instrument (trumpet), whose sound we amplified using the same technique. The sound of the trumpet and guitars, produced in this manner, created a psychedelic effect whose unusual quality intensified the experience even more. Even here we made use of kettledrums, which became an indispensable instrument at the band's subsequent concerts.

The concert was at the end of April, one Friday evening: chilly winds were already blowing in the street. Before the performance, a bandmate and I went over to the Holy Trinity statue, because we were waiting for our friends, and watched the arriving crowd. Somehow I felt that I had to file this image away somewhere inside me, because already the strange anticipation radiating from the new arrivals had an effect on me, all by itself. The audience's ages at this concert spanned several generations, from teenagers to youths in their thirties to older people. In the back rows the older people appeared, which gave me a strange feeling at the time. It was clear that among these people were some internal security agents, who had recruited some sneaky informants from among the younger crowd. We weren't afraid of them, since it was immediately apparent who didn't belong there and who was trying to hang onto us in an odd way and ask stupid questions. Moreover, we had nothing to be afraid of, since they couldn't have interfered with anything we were doing.

That was already our second concert that week, a rare occurrence. The previous concert had been at the Budapest University of Economics

Experimental Studio, where we may have succeeded even more at immersing ourselves in the experience of free music-making, in accordance with the Experimental Studio's expectations. It surprised us how well the concert went; as a result, we were filled with new and special energies. Bolstered by these, we arrived at this second concert, where many more people had appeared and where we ended up performing for a full house.

Interestingly, this time there was no opening band or other production, just our performance. The large hall was full on this chilly April evening. We went up on stage, and a strange connection with the audience took hold. As always, we felt that we were about to be part of a special musical experience, which we would then transmit with good feeling to everyone. Invisible spiritual scanners went into operation, and our internal sources came to the surface. This boundless, free experience was accompanied by a shared trust, which ensured the meeting of souls. It was clear that, choosing boundless freedom at this concert, we were leaping into the world of unknown sounds; communicating without words, we would offer our audience some kind of special experience. The boundaries between fantasy and reality were blurred by sounds and associated images. The act of bringing fantasy to life combined with an experience of freedom, which offered joy, the magic of childlike wonderment. It was important to us to create an atmosphere where even the stiffest audience member's fantasy would take off, so that this person, too, would want to be part of this shared experience.

The sounds and images started to build, and then the journey began, consisting of the following images. We are gliding along with the listeners in the corridors of a cave, everyone in a common body, like an enormous, invisible stream. Karst waters are leaking through the cracks, gleaming in the light of the smoking torches; we feel the water flowing onto our faces. The smell of earth wafts from the passages, and the cold weighs on our lungs as we rush. White-winged angels swoop down at the sound of our footsteps; snatching them, we glide with great speed toward the light of the exit. Mist hisses from the nostrils of unbridled horses. Horns and trombones blare inside the deafening sound of hooves, and giant bolts of lightning zigzag across the cliffs, from where a mist of rapids and waterfalls spreads across the landscape. As the hooves recede, the hush fills our souls with peace....

These and similar images accompanied our music. What the band members encountered together, the listeners experienced as well. The images accompanying the musical process, and their impulses, were transposed to those in the room. At the end of the concert, the stunned silence indicated that the show had succeeded; a few seconds later, this silence was followed by the usual applause, screams, and other sound effects. Our experiences corresponded with those of the audience.

As music is made, a strange current starts moving on the waves of the imagination and plays on the strings of the emotions. A warm wave of emotion, bringing happiness, floods our interior, raising our endorphin level. This is the way it almost always works, regardless of whether we transmit wild and cathartic things, or beautiful, heartbreaking cascades of sound. Once we reach such a moment, the current rushes onward inside us with overwhelming force. We feel our heart and soul opening up; we sense that we have been given the intoxicating experience of illusion. One may ask whether it is in fact an illusion that we encounter here. The joy of boundless freedom is a strange, unfamiliar wave of emotion.

During our music-making, in the trance state we lived, our normal, everyday perceptions of space and time, our interpretation of cause-and-effect relationships, and our functions of perception were transformed or erased. In this state, everything that is impossible seems self-evident and is conveyed with a much more definite sense of reality than under ordinary conditions. At our concerts, the images and image series that we received during internal transformation appeared and disappeared at once with timeless speed. The images do not appear one after the other according to customary worldly time; instead, they all move and exist almost simultaneously, together. They do not proceed as a still image; rather, as the events are taking place, experienced time does not go by. I take up the explanation later in the book, in more detail, when introducing relativistic brain function. These processes and phenomena, coupled with the spiritual encounter and internal picturing that emerge from the brain's work, are caused not by reflex reactions to bodily perception of the external world, but rather by an inner transformation separate from and not directly connected to the material at hand.

Music created in this way provided spiritual depth, through which musical performance, transformed into a lived and communal experience.

I believe and affirm that music-creation based on internal picturing was the band's unique and universal discovery.

This musical performance, by fulfilling our faith in it, created an internal experience that affected our souls; it was accompanied, in magical elegance, by musical wildness and raw force.

Bringing our soul into action helps us fulfil our inner psyche, which is essential, because with our psyche we can influence our body and its functioning. Noetic energy put to work by the soul is capable of changing our life processes, breathing, blood pressure, metabolism, and other functions of our organs. Our psyche has yet another special characteristic, which is that it can separate from our body, leaving it in a lifeless state, and then return to it. It can transgress the classical laws of physics, such as gravity, and cross boundaries of space and time. The psyche is capable of building the body; a force lies in thought, which is able to alter material and bring it into being.

The trance state that emerged during music-making—we can also call it an altered state of consciousness—created a perfect syntonic state within us. This meant an expanded conscious and ecstatic experience. The music was paired with an exceptional and unique, freestyle form of dancing, carried out by our singer and the several guitarists; in this dance, movements arose spontaneously, from within; through the music and musicians, the inner essence of the human being was expressed, suggesting to us that our higher self had revealed itself. This was the experience of inner transformation, intensified by the ecstatic beat of the music; we felt ourselves identifying with the entire world, the universe. This is a kind of intellectual adventure that we are incapable of judging until we have experienced it. The image streams, gushing along with the music, provoked a powerful sense of safety and euphoria, as if we had experienced eternal life, independent of space and time.

I have given much thought to this special emotional cascade and tried to find its root. This powerful sense of safety and communal experience, leading to a feeling of pleasure, proceeds from an internal source so strong that it relegates everything else to the background. This source is the force of the soul, which, if we mobilize it, comes with an all-encompassing, undirected experience of happiness. Based on the experiences during our concerts, this shared spiritual experience overflowed with love in an interesting way. It is no surprise that the audience members loved the band and each other, a feeling that continued to be generated afterward. We did not need media support or advertisements, since without them everything worked, almost on its own, as the bases were strong and genuine.

To those who have not had a similar experience, or who doubt what I have tried to describe and convey so far, I recommend this ten-minute musical excerpt, available through the QR code below, of the Kinizsi Street concert that we gave in 1985.

This show was held in the courtyard of a university dormitory, where about a thousand people came together. Several alternative bands performed that spring evening. We were announced as a surprise, though I believe news of the event had already spread by word of mouth throughout the entire city. I recommend listening to the concert excerpt with closed eyes, in the kind of relaxed and balanced state where our interior becomes receptive to discovering a world foreign to us, experiencing its beauties and wild powers. Everyone should try to give himself over to the effect, even if the musical and sound experiences on the recording are not what you are used to. The inspiration given by a cavalcade of natural effects and whale sounds, together with the effect created by shaking and amplifying a two-square-meter steel plate, provided a huge space for completing the musical world. Whoever listens several times to this music, built from within and born there, in that moment—actually an authentic impression of that evening and the transcendent force field present there—will find that its essence becomes clearer and clearer, and that special energy that I am trying to write about in this book will come across more easily. When we gave this concert, we did not know where the path would lead us; we just proceeded from chaos into the realm of order, then from order into the realm of infinite chaos. In the meantime, everything before us became clear and complete, and before the audience too. Everything found its place in this process; the created spiritual force field freed the usual reflex barriers, both in our brains and in our souls. In this noetic and spiritual force field, every sound had a place; there was no sour note, no unfitting sound or rhythm. This was a production generated completely from within and created together with the audience, where we the musicians, as each other's and the audience's mediums, brought to the surface, in musical form, the spiritual result of shared involvement. It is important, during listening, to try to set aside the thinking technique forced upon us by everyday life and to release our psyche, which our rational thought has halted. This opening will bring out immense positive energy and inquisitive internal potential.

With this I have tried to put into words those internal experiences that I live again now, thinking back and listening again to the recording. The musical excerpt consists of the last ten minutes of an approximately hour-long concert; it confirms that the band created and applied suggestive, free creation based on spontaneously realized internal picturing. It was entirely like this at the concert: the music was born spontaneously in the moment, and we played it only then, there, unrepeatably. This was not a repertory song or an improvisation building on a practiced template, but truly organic music, born out of the relationship between the band members and the special spiritual identification with the audience. As I have already stressed, on a sound recording only a small fraction of what we experienced can come across, since the suggestive effect's carrying force, causing shared involvement, cannot come about without the presence of brain waves in the shared space or the meeting of souls. Even so, I thought that it would have a strong effect. Naturally the transmission of images and the resultant atmosphere do not come across here either as they would among the crowd, but a listener can follow the musical realization of the entire experience.

The Human Brain's Relativistic Time Perception and Operation

As I highlighted in the introduction, this book's particular value is that it sheds light on the capacities and potential of our brain function in relativistic conditions.

At concerts I noticed that I experienced elapsed time in a different way during the performance. This meant that I perceived the passage of time as faster than it actually was. Actually, we encounter this sensation often and in many ways during our daily lives. I will now take up this set of questions in somewhat more detail and interpret the experience, its background, and its consequences in relation to artistic creative process or scientific activity. In my opinion, the human brain is capable of working in a relativistic manner; as this does not happen in the customary, everyday dimension of time and space, this process allows us to receive experiences that create a kind of illusion before which we stand almost bewildered. In our scientific and definitive world based on everyday experiences, we don't know what to make of such encounters. I've tried to map out the relevant current research on the subject, but no such approach has really been formulated, especially not with an empirical basis. During our concerts, as I have mentioned, we had many visionary experiences; the effect, radiated in the music, of our image-based conceptions created a special illusion. How this might relate to the relativistic functioning capabilities of our brain, I will try to explain in the following pages with my own theory and the inferences derived from my experiences. I will begin by suggesting that every person has some kind of relation to existence outside of space and time. We have concepts such as eternity, infinity or immortality, psyche, soul, which we come to know and grasp as small children through folk tales, because the ancients left these behind for us. These are not concepts that our real, actual senses can detect and comprehend, yet we can grapple with them in some way.

With regard to the human brain's time perception, an interesting fact can be established. Everyone has the experience that days lived out in childhood seem longer than the same length of time experienced at an older age. It seems that the older we get, the faster time goes by.

According to another perception, if we are bored or have nothing to do and feel superfluous, then time goes by more slowly than when events spin by, or we are occupied with something that interests us greatly.

It has also been observed that those ill with a fever perceive time as faster. Those who perform regular artistic and scientific activities always seem younger and more youthful. Music-making that comes from internal intuition results in a similar time perception. An interesting piece of reading or scientific activity also speeds up subjective time perception; that is, we perceive the passage of time as faster. This means that our subjective inner clock goes more slowly; thus, we perceive the actual time of our external world as passing more quickly. According to Einstein's special theory of relativity, time in a moving system, when viewed from a system at rest, goes more slowly. These two effects are, of course, relative, and each observer, moving relative to the other, will find that the other's distances, measured in his own system, will contract slightly in the direction of motion, and that the other's clock will run more slowly. Similarly, time in a standing or slow system, perceived from a moving, fast system, goes by faster.

As we grow older, we feel subjectively that time is going faster; the years, months, and days pass by faster. Relativistic time perception is at work here too, since when we get older, our brain processes the experiences acquired over a lifetime, and—according to a vivid expression in our language—the multitude of experienced images "experientializes" itself and becomes an experience in itself, and thus gets stored in the stream of our lives. Things that we never paid attention to but that somehow affected us, and that we do not consciously remember, stay inside us as image patches. While our everyday brain is capable of guiding us between finite frames, the areas controlled by the right brain hemisphere, severed from our conscious thought, make it possible for us, reaching beyond our limits, to use the images stored away in our infinite warehouse, in our own way. This enables an image-making mechanism to work inside us unconsciously, making use of our memories and the things we have learned and allowing us to experience things that we perhaps cannot recall consciously. As we grow older, our set of stored images grows larger; as a result, our internal picturing and imagination are able to draw on an ever-richer warehouse. As we age, we become more and more experienced, we grow wiser in all areas of life, we see through the workings of the surrounding world better and better, and matters of greater complexity become clear. The brain's neurons work upon and transmit an ever larger set. It takes more and more energy to scan an ever-growing set of images and to generate and combine particular image elements; the brain neuron's speed also increases because of the increased quantity of data being stored and processed. As a result, our internal clock seems slower, while our perception of external time quickens. This process is almost imperceptible, forming inside us over many years; sometimes it takes us by surprise.

When we sleep and dream, we likewise sense upon waking that the night flew by. In that case the process is much quicker; that is, the effect can be felt not after years have gone by, but after just a few hours. The state of sleep is similar to that of hypnosis; that is, the brain functions differently than it would normally. This is equally true for meditation or relaxed-state hypnosis as for active waking hypnosis, for instance, when athletes' performance can be further intensified.

During our concerts, on many occasions, we experienced this subjective passage of time; that is, we perceived the actually elapsed time period as faster. Beyond this, we perceived other, seemingly inexplicable effects, which at the time we were not fully able to see through and explain. In such a state, the perception of outside time is faster, the brain neurons' speed increases, and our internal clock seems slower; moreover, according to experimental measurements, the nerve centers' energy is greater. The facts of Einstein's special theory of relativity can be shown and verified in instances where the moving bodies approach the speed of light, but at everyday speeds, these relativistic changes are immeasurably small. However, our thoughts are capable of great speeds; the speed of brain neurons' motion presumably allows for such speeds where the effects of relativistic time perception come into play.

Research has demonstrated, for instance, that the meditative state accelerates brain function. Consequently, it can be assumed that brain function accelerates similarly in the hypnotic state.

In an altered state of consciousness, brain function changes. In various studies, it has been shown that in the state of hypnosis, reality check decreases, the sense of time changes, emotional experience and expression become livelier. Cognitive functioning becomes more intuitive and creative, while the change of time perception, and the internal experience of it, becomes an essential element of the process.

The human brain has some 100 billion (1E+11) neurons. Every single neuron generates about 100–200 outputs per second, and every neuron is connected to about 1,000 other neurons. To give a sense of the scale, if we modeled the human brain as a simple neural net, then it would be equivalent to a computer capable of executing 1E+16 operations per second (that is, 1E+16 bit/s). If all our neurons were operating, which means that if our brain were being used to full capacity, this would correspond to a frequency of 1E+16 Hz, which would theoretically enable us to think at frequencies above the frequency of visible light (3.9E+14 – 7.8E+14 Hz). There is research that estimates the frequency of the subconscious mind at 3.2E+11 Hz. Many studies deal with the human brain and especially with determining the neuron speed arising during subconscious brain function, and more and more results and hypotheses reinforce the idea that this activity—primarily in the subconscious regions—approaches the speed of light.

Since for most people the left brain hemisphere is much more dominant, it is particularly important to bring the right brain hemisphere to the appropriate level of functioning. According to some research, the rationally functioning left brain hemisphere can handle about 2000 bit/s of information, whereas the right hemisphere is responsible for about 400 billion bit/s (4E+11 Hz).

The realization of archaic transcendent knowledge can take place through self-suggestion, or through suggestion between two parties, or group/mass suggestion. In such a state, the human brain processes information with greater speed and energy than in its everyday workings. On the basis of Einstein's energy-mass transformation, we already know that not only does energy have mass, but energy can be transformed into mass, and mass into energy. He had already assumed, and later others verified through experiments, that this interrelation between energy and mass applies to all types of energy.

This can serve as a basis for understanding the image-driven, energy-generating effect of mental concentration, and can also help explain, in today's terms, those supernatural, extraordinary phenomena that are often referred to as occult and mystical. This may include the instance of a person under deep hypnosis who has been informed that he is touching a glowing piece of iron while in fact a piece of wood is being pressed into his hand, and who then develops burns on his skin. Similar is the show of those Far Eastern masters, the fakirs, which modern science is unable to explain: the teacher tells a story, which the spectators plastically see and experience, even though nothing actually happens. With the force of his imagination, the performer is able to bring everyone to see what he sees. Of course, our imagination is capable of affecting others only within a certain circle. The capacity for internal picturing is inside us, but this works to different degrees depending on our personality and our specific mental potential.

Inasmuch as we accept the applications and laws of Einstein's special theory of relativity as it pertains to our brain function, the phenomenon of space-time transformation is true for our brain function as well. This means that within certain limits, the concept of space is interchangeable with that of time, and vice versa. Simply explained, this means that in a system moving close to the speed of light, events occurring in the same place (for example, in the brain of the stunt performer) but at different times are perceived as events in different places by a stationary or slower-moving observer.

Following the principle of space-time transformation, we can rephrase the previous statement by exchanging the words "place" (space) and "time" with each other. We then arrive at the concept that in a fast-moving system (say, in the brain of the stunt performer), events occurring at the same time but in different places are seen and felt by a stationary or slower-moving observer as events taking place at different times. It has further been established that the time difference between two simultaneous events of one system as displayed in the other system is related to the shortened distances between the events. The first concept has the result that in a moving system, time perceived from a system at rest goes by more slowly.

At our concerts, I too had several sensual illusions and visions during the entire experience of the music flow, as did as my fellow musicians; those in attendance often reported similar experiences. These are illusions caused by the distortion of space and time, which affect our perception of time and space. The stronger the involvement, the greater the possible distortion of time and space perception. This is the result of the intensified image processing of our brain function, which, because of relativistic time perception, subjectively alters not only our time perception, but also our perception of space and distance.

In our brain's trance state, or during another activity that comes with enhanced noetic image-making, our thought process is transferred to a different coordinate system, that is, a different system of reference, from the usual earthly coordinate system. External signs of this are manifested, for instance, as an intensified internal state, a stronger heartbeat, or the reverse: the pulse can become slower in the case of meditation. In both cases the point is that we end up in a different coordinate system, from which standpoint our perception of earthly physical laws changes. Dimensions, times, and time-shifts open up new perspectives to us. Our relation with matter and nature is transformed; it takes on a different form, and we come into possession of new forces as a result of the mutual effect. At such times, it is essential for us to somehow step out of our usual, earthly biological rhythms. Our brain function makes this possible, and with the development of our internal picturing capacity, it becomes reachable and achievable. Individuals who perform strong noetic activities can experience this effect on their own: for instance, after immersive work or activity, when they perceive the elapsed time as faster than usual.

It also follows that if we accept, during our everyday lives, such relativistic behavior as can be experienced in the perception of time, then scientific findings on the perception of space and time offer an interesting basis for understanding some of our seemingly inexplicable observations. I do not wish to delve further into the discussion of the special theory of relativity, but perhaps in the future, phenomena such as telepathy or other intuitions, the transfer of images, the placebo effect, and the feeling of déjà vu can be explained through these hypotheses.

Reactions experienced in hypnotic states of differing depth, as well as seemingly inexplicable phenomena, can be attributed to the brain's relativistic function that has been stimulated in that state.

However, the goal of this book is not to analyze the various manifestations of the psyche's and soul's function or their energy states in scientific terms; rather, I try to point out those scientific possibilities whose principles allow us to handle properly the hypotheses and experiences we have accrued up to now.

Perceiving a fuller picture of the world, and gaining the capacity for this, can lead to the acquisition and use of magical knowledge. To date, the great discoveries, inventions, scientific results, and stunning artistic creations have drawn on this special capacity of ours, since they came into being through the application of transcendent knowledge arising from the soul and formed by our internal psyche. One might say that the involvement of the soul in our noetic actions creates and assists relativistic brain function, allowing us to achieve things of great consequence and transmit them to others, even without using words. Assisted by the balance of our intellectual and spiritual brain function, we can create truly great and enduring things. The lack of one or the other disrupts the unity and harmony of our relationship to the world.

Music and the Fundamental Principles of Hypnosis

In a few scholarly books I sought information about the mechanism and workings of ancient transcendent knowledge, which I had mapped out through experience as described earlier. I came to the conclusion that hypnosis comes closest to what I had experienced, and within it, self-hypnosis and self-suggestion. Self-hypnosis can develop outward into group or mass hypnosis, depending on how deeply and effectively the self-hypnosis practitioners can work. Namely, we experience and use hypnosis almost every day on ourselves, as well as on those living in our midst.

During our performances, we sometimes carried this out quite successfully. In those days, we were not yet aware of the principles and function of the process that had been realized; we just felt their magic and effect. The explanation of the experience, and the conclusions that can be drawn from it, came together into a unity only much later; I will try to summarize them here.

Various scholarly works discuss hypnosis's working mechanism, as well as fundamental principles; among these, I have tried to find those that best fit the experiences of our musical activity, providing insight into the function and thus enabling us to recognize and appropriately handle the consciousness-altering effects that touch us throughout our lives. In the following pages I will try to introduce these principles with the support of experiences gained over the course of our music-creating process.

On the basis of scholarly works that deal with hypnosis, the most important foundational principle is that all our internal picturing strives for realization. In the case of the band, that meant that before every concert we discussed what images we were thinking of, and as soon as we went on stage, the same picture appeared in each of our heads. For instance, a mountain collapsed right in front of us, and a waterfall poured with enormous energy into the valley. We had to convey this image through the music. We took this seriously and believed in it. On the plane of thought, we reached a dimension where we felt the crowd, the occurrences of the evening. When we tuned to the audience's and each other's resonances, a special emotional and spiritual connection took hold. We felt the exceptional atmosphere on stage; the crowd's eyes were fixed on us, the anticipation and the impulses created some kind of special experience in us. In the meantime, the image started to come to life in us, and the music sounded forth. Willy-nilly, a process of implementation took off. In the world, we cannot bring anything into being or destroy anything; at most we can transform. There is one exception: thought. Through it, we can conjure anything out of nothing; that is, thought can emerge from within us into reality. When this thought, condensed into image, is accompanied by a strong desire for implementation, then nothing can prevent it from becoming real. The desire was supported by the music and accompanying sound effects, which helped to express the images contained in thought, make them almost plastic, and project them to others.

The second foundational principle is the opposition of will and faith. If these two come face to face, faith will always prevail. This is crucial. If we want to go to sleep, but meanwhile think that we can't fall asleep, then in fact we will not be able. In contrast, if we imagine ourselves falling asleep, then we will, because we believe that it will happen. The same applies to healing. Our wish to be healed is in vain if we do not believe that we will heal. Faith has tremendous power. There are those who put all their strength into attaining their goals, yet their wanting it so badly does not lead them to success. Addictions also show the victory of faith (or lack thereof) over will, when the person struggling with addiction cannot get rid of a harmful passion because he believes more in the thing that made him addicted than in recovery.

Many bands want to make good music. But if they do not believe that they can do so, or if they don't even bother because they are not aware of the relationship between faith and will, then nothing will come of it, just hacking.

The pendulum experiment is a good example of the relation between faith and will. If we hold a pendulum between two of our fingers and do not want our hand to move but believe that the pendulum will, then, precisely because we have imagined that, the pendulum will move, because faith is always victorious over the will. This is important, because when we played, we believed what we were doing and experiencing. The band let the second fundamental principle take effect; that is, we believed in the transformation of visually conceived and formulated musical images into a shared experience, and we wished to realize this on stage.

In the band's golden era, we believed in our friendship, we believed that we saw the same experiential images, and that we could display them through the music, live them out, and give this experience to the audience. The connection and strength of our souls was multiplied through this.

This is quite a bold undertaking, since at the moment when faith is shaken, wonder and its magic come to an end. For this to happen, it is enough for one band member to falter. The chain is as strong as its weakest link.

The third fundamental principle is the generation of an opposing force through exertion. Intentional exertion supported by faith is in vain if not accompanied by imagination in the form of imagery; not only does it go nowhere, but it will have an effect in the opposite direction and will fail. This is why if a weak and a strong person face each other, and the big muscular colossus wants to defeat the smaller one, but the latter believes (through imagining) that he can overcome him, then he will win. If we would like to attain something through the will alone, then it will backfire. The energy potential of the person approaching with faith is doubled, since with his faith he already increases his own energy, while his opponent's energy is countered due to the effort of the will.

The same thing happened at some of our very weak concerts. If one of us had his faith shaken, or one of us was startled out of the phase of visualization and internal experience, then the effect did not take place; in fact, the production became clumsy and rattling, so the stunning experience never happened. In contrast, at our successful concerts, because of the fundamental principles discussed previously, the faith realized through strong image-making was able to create immense energy in the crowd, through the power of the soul. This confirms that the application of archaic transcendent knowledge has creative power.

It follows that our thoughts do not just exist freely and unnoticed in our lives, since every thought has a specific effect and magic. This principle is also essential in the case of mass hypnosis: if some skeptics do not want to accept the suggestions, or even oppose them, then the image transformation accompanied by strong faith, which the majority of the crowd has already embraced, will cause the involvement of these individuals as well. Thus the creative force goes into action, since their will

will have a negative effect, yet our transferring energy potential will consequently become stronger. This happened at our successful concerts.

While the band was at work, music was definitely the medium for applying the principles. Through the transmission of faith, it ensured the activation of the soul. It is interesting that modern science is incapable of defining music coherently. Nonetheless, it can be established that music has a unique effect on the brain with respect to learning, memory, and the soul. Performing, listening to, or composing music is perhaps the activity that requires the most cognitive skills. It can have such a powerful effect as to lead soldiers to war, make dancers and listeners fall into ecstasy or an altered state of consciousness, or assist meditation.

According to recent research, the brain centers associated with reward and addiction are specifically stimulated when we listen to new, unfamiliar music.

Sounds affect the emotions, recollections, and memory in a unique way. Rhythm also plays a very important role in music, especially when intensified by drums. Rhythm has another, profound effect on the brain; it has a powerful influence on perception, emotion, and thought. It has been observed that during deep sleep, sounds played to a slow drumbeat intensify the memory and recollection. Brain activity during the creation of musical improvisations has been linked to brain activity during sleep and meditation. Music is used during various spiritual practices, meditations and prayers. Here the sounds, melody, repeated rhythm, and internal images play an essential role. They enable the absorption of the active mind in order to attain an experience beyond thought. According to research, during spiritual exercises, movements and rhythm have a highly positive effect on both the immune system and the cognitive function. One can play powerful music and improvise in a special trance state of the brain, similar to REM (rapid eye movement), the trance state of the sleep phase in which dreams are born.

The trance state that develops during creation can be considered partial, since our consciousness is also available at the same moment in time.

Each branch of the arts chooses and applies different paths toward expressive inner imagery.

Music differs from painting or theater, for instance, in that it does not have a direct visual reference. Thus, during music-making or listening, the visual brain areas are also used less.

Since music is a feeling, our limbic system is activated by the auditory centers. The feeling emerges from the musician's authentic essence. All authentic and cathartic art is a form of the creator's authenticity expressed through his internal picturing process and imagination. A musician's brain reflects the creation of music and creates a trance state.

It is worth noting that internal picturing not only applies to the attainment of meditation, but can be an important building block for any creative process. During concerts, our band used this internal picturing as one of the steps of archaic transcendent magical knowledge. The altered state of consciousness attained through our music is a meditative state, which can affect people and evoke a trance state in an active, alert way. Although today internal picturing is primarily associated with meditation, I am convinced that it can be interpreted and used much more broadly, that is, it can be applied during sports, life, and creative processes just as in art.

At our successful concerts it became clear that the matters of our lives are not only decided in the world of rigid logic limited by definitions, or through selfish interests, but also through the boundless paths of the soul. Perhaps these resonances aroused by true feeling provided the basis and suggestion for our ever growing camp of fans. As a result of the concert experiences, the limitations and errors of the world could be compared, in the souls of the fans, with the true forces of infinite spiritual freedom and unmanipulated purity. This particular experience was coupled with an additional perception that could be realized through the mediation of spiritual energy. A crucial and forgotten ancient truth came wordlessly to the surface, namely, that the soul cannot be misled; that is, it cannot be manipulated. This explains how in a strong suggestive state we have access to deep, internal, hidden, and inherited matters that we bear as a heavy burden and carry onward. Beyond this, perceiving the horizons of the infinite through our relative brain function also offers an experience that is usually called a spiritual, sacred encounter, because it cannot yet be interpreted through the deductive, justificatory nature of today's science. Perhaps with this explanation, strictly materialistic thinkers can grasp the concept of spirituality and the empirical encounter with archaic spiritual experiences.

Let us now consider the limits into which our personalities are forced through repeated playing or listening to today's trendy music or a precisely repeated artistic performance. This squeezes both the performers and the viewers and listeners into narrow limits that leave no room for the experience of infinity or the perception of challenging, unforeseen possibilities. A learning mechanism encoded in humans allows us to reach results through repetitions and practice. It is difficult to extract our psyches from this treadmill, and so we would rather enjoy familiar situations and activities and gratefully hum familiar melodies. This script is unable to activate our spiritual capacities and gives no space to the intuition. We must necessarily reach the recesses of the soul where we can live out the magic of the infinite and the fortuitous, and we must dare to perceive this. With the band, making room for this bold undertaking, we realized that we were trying to mine the unexpected possibilities of the infinite. The performance of a practiced thing cannot offer an internal experience on a scale like that of choosing experientially from the immense set of infinite possibilities, and living out its magic, which we can bring to life on the wings of our souls, and which actually is nothing other than what we believe through our internal picturing.

Let us consider that a defining part of today's entertainment-oriented music consists of repetition. This is true for the lyrics as well. This squeezes humans' internal world into a narrow frame; that is, it does not give any opportunity for living out broader experiences. Classical music, defined in the narrowest sense, still lived with the possibility of omitting this type of simplistic repetition and making room for broader and ever broadening musical processes. And truly, these works affect us more profoundly; it is no accident that they are timeless.

Ancient Magical Knowledge
Preserved in the Hungarian Language

It is important for us to see that our language preserves, at many levels, the knowledge of ancient magic. Through the Hungarian language, we think in images; the language's pictorial nature testifies to its antiquity. The perceptible origin of abstract concepts arising from observation of natural phenomena is less obscured here than in other languages. Within Hungarian, an exceptional image-making force is exhibited. Through thinking in images, we "get the picture." We see the whole, everything that we need to know about a given matter; this is closely related to magical knowledge. In our language we use word-images, which help us display images in the most effective way possible, bring our fantasy to life, and express our spiritual resonances plastically. These days it has become quite fashionable to appropriate words from English-language professional literature. Granted, a comparison of professional English with the whole of Hungarian is bound to be imbalanced; that said, I find the latter much more expressive than the former, especially in its use of roots. For instance, I prefer to use the phrase *belső **kép**alkotás* ("internal picturing") instead of *imagináció* ("imagination"). We need only consider how plastically our words ***kép**zelet* ("imagination") and ***kép**esség* ("capability, ability") express their meanings, both deriving from *kép* ("image"). We are "capable" (***kép**esek*) of achieving, with complete success, something that we want to achieve, if we "envision" (*el**kép**zeljük*) it in its entirety.

Our word ***kép**zés* ("training") also suggests that the image-based transfer of knowledge provides the essentials for all sorts of knowledge acquisition. Well and appropriately "trained" (***kép**zett*) people move the chariot of our world forward. They suggest that learning and its acquisition and application require thinking and reasoning in images.

The synthesis of our musical sounds and our linguistic expressions, when it hits the mark, has an effect similar to resonance; that is, when the frequency of the element causing the excitation and that of the excited element converge, an increase in energy results. Thus, we can increase the effectiveness of the internal image display by expressing the sounds and empirically perceived content with visual words.

For further examples, we can examine our words *átélés* ("profoundly lived experience") or *tapasztalat* ("empirical experience"), which fully express and describe what they mean (átélés literally means "through-living"; *tapasztalat* may derive from the dialectical verb *tapaszt ~ patch,* "knowledge stamped on us" or "knowledge patched on us"). I do not believe that other languages can express these meanings so well, and in such a way, with a single word.

In Hungarian, our word *szer* ("tool, order, method, layer, measure, substance, ceremony, proportion, substance") has made quite an interesting mark, which we use in a variety of contexts. Examples include, but are not limited to: **szer**elem ("romantic or sexual love"), **szer**etet ("familial love, affection, fondness"), **szer**tartás ("ceremony"), kény**szer** ("compulsion"), gyógy**szer** ("medicine"). Our ancestors recognized the omnipotent power of love. Their relationship with God is *szer*, which **szer**ez ("obtains, creates") and **szer**et ("loves") in the rend**szer** ("system") of the whole world. This also preserves our language's hidden and profoundly archaic logic. Ancient ceremonies conveyed love to the participants. Our ancestors' vér**szer**ződés ("blood contract") was also an important milestone in our past. The root *szer* thus expresses a spiritual quality, not a material one: a nourishing, creative, positive, even healing force.

One of my favorite expressions is *kezelés* ("management, handling, treatment"), which derives from *kéz* ("hand"). In truth, long ago, people cured others through laying on hands; our language preserves this ancient magic.

I would like to digress to the question of why I consider language an important magical element, be it any language spoken in the world. In the band's golden era, we introduced many slang words that ended up in colloquial language. Such was the word *csákó*, meaning "guy, dude, bloke," or the verb *parádézni* ("to express overflowing joy"). Similarly, we invented the expression *sirály* (literally, "seagull") as a synonym for *király* (literally "king," but also slang for "cool, great"). I have always been interested in the mechanism through which a word ends up in common speech. For instance, a few years ago, the use of the expression *úgymond* ("they say") became very popular. It's used everywhere and has already become slightly annoying. In fact, the mechanism of word adoption has to do with some kind of subconscious suggestion, which affects us instinctively and continues onward among us. The question, then, is what triggers the suggestion.

In active waking hypnosis, repetition—an activity rendered nearly monotonous, which intensifies the suggestion—plays an essential role. We need hardly pay attention to it; it works automatically. But perhaps the brain's mirror neurons play a role in its formation. As a band, we often applied the magic of repetition in music, but in such a way that we always slightly changed the repeated musical passages so that the music would have the quality of something in formation and would assist its associated image progress in time and space, that is, to change and develop. Word-images, similes, and other stylistic devices used in Hungarian can support our imaginings and utterances quite plastically. Our storehouse is immense, and our language, with its *magyarázó* ("explanatory") nature, supplies an effective backdrop to thought occurring in images.

Perhaps because of the capabilities of our language, we think in images more easily and convey matters more expressively than do speakers of other languages. Consider our famous poets' brilliant poems, which are not simple to translate into other languages. That is, our language's particularities make us especially capable of mobilizing our internal picturing capacity (though each language has its particular gifts).

Based on my experience, the appropriate activation of the soul with its vast power triggered effective suggestions. One can attain such activation by bringing to life a faith evoked through strong internal picturing. Consider our word *lelkiismeret* ("conscience," "spiritual representative," literally "spiritual knowledge"). This alludes to the knowledge of the soul: that is, when someone accomplishes something that proceeds from the soul, it becomes worthy of recognition. Honor and respect derive from this, among other things. Our soul is the source of exclusively good things; a healthy soul engenders love. Perhaps the soul is the seed of life; it is no coincidence that the ancients used to say, when someone died, that he breathed out his soul. Our soul is the key to expanding our noetic function, with the experiences received through internal picturing and with the help of faith. The wonder of the infinite, combined with the magic of wordless communication, makes our minds capable of conveying and receiving various internal experiences and effects. That is, the carrier is the soul itself.

In the band's defining years, we used the forces preserved in our language primarily to specify to each other, in the most detailed way, extending to every particular, our emotions' secret oscillations and our spiritual states. During this practice, it happened that we told each other about the effect of the great volumes of music that we listened to together, the experience it offered, describing it in images. Our singer, who could plastically convey internal experiences, was the master of this. This was intensified by our listening to certain songs many times in a row; the joy of deeper recognition, hidden inside repetition, intensified the entire process. Perhaps this was the step that led us to the true experience of transformation through music, and allowed us to attain recognition of the effect's secrets. From this emerged the building of the important and defining foundation stones of our improvisational concerts and our internal recording, in advance, of these concerts in images.

Our Company's Amusing Internal Visualization Exercises for an Unmade Film

From the preceding pages it can be established and perceived that the Hungarian language powerfully supports our internal picturing process. This might even be considered one of the defining characteristics of our language.

As I have mentioned several times already, our company of friends was characterized not only by its uniquely realized musical creative process, but by unbridled cheer and, along with this, the merry procession, which on a few occasions burst into choking laughter. At such times we explained a certain phrase and its different meanings to each other. The suggestive effect led us all to fall over with laughter at the end. The point was to see who, following an emotional urge, could react most strikingly to a given expression. In retrospect, what mattered in these great moments was who could think in images, and at what depth, and express it, convey it to the others. If a bold and interesting image flashed inside one of us, and this person told a story about it, then the others, attuning themselves to this, seeing and experiencing the same series of images, would continue the narration, making its pictorial effect more and more interesting. We nearly cut into each other's words; that is how the most astonishing and rampant, effective and funny statements spilled out of us. After a little while, we realized that an interesting film could be made of this. From then on, at these gatherings, we always produced the material and refined the individual stories for our film.

The boundless freedom of tight and true friendship made room for this strange, cheer-inducing experience. Perhaps we are still game for such togetherness today.

Besides our unusual musical creative mode, it may also have helped that we were attracted to avant-garde artistic works; Buñuel's films in particular had a great influence on us. Perhaps I could compare the images that we experienced and built together during the lively entertainment described in the preceding pages to Buñuel's film *Un chien andalou*.

In our company of friends, over time, many such image streams, particular to us, were born: the pictorial idea-crumbs for a film that never got made. Our company consisted first and foremost of the band's stalwart members, then the members of the ritual movement theater and a few close friends. However, I would highlight the active participation, in this process, of the families' younger generation, who as adults enthusiastically participate in the further refinement of the script.

These friendly gatherings mainly took place on summer evenings in the Balaton highlands or the banks of the Körös river, along with wine-drinking, accompanied with good music, under an old walnut tree, where the internal cinema stretched into the night. Its frenetic power had a great effect on all of us. The individual scenes were naturally of a silent film sort, whose pictorial force swept human fantasy along with it. For our content, we used the fantasy impressions that sprang from our company of friends' oblivious, terrific cheer and unbridled merriment. This was such a secret thread between us that it felt good to share it, and like a kind of creative process, it offered true emotional and spiritual reinforcement. In that state, ending up on the same wavelength, we saw almost the same series of internal images; reinforcing each other, these took form and shape. I think that in this book I cannot acquaint the reader with these sets of ideas, since they are not my independent thoughts, but the result of a shared creative process; thus everyone's consent would be needed. But I will pick one among them, to give at least a sense of the image-making process and its result, which I have tried to describe.

Work Film Excerpt

Tall mountain peaks around us, blazing summer and sparkling sunshine. Our friend, who is actually all but Clint's alter ego, in battered, dusty leather boots, jeans, sánd an unbuttoned, faded plaid shirt, stumbles with a strange gait through the bleak countryside toward the Rocky Mountains. He seems bald, but interestingly, his grey hair falls from the back of his head down to his shoulders. This is because he has forced a bald wig onto his head, and his locks stick out beneath it. He wears special seven-league boots, with especially bright, huge spurs. When he reaches the foot of the mountain range, he hops in his boots from one peak to the next; with each leap, the rock beneath his spurs sparkles. When he leaps a kilometer, everything gets cloaked in dust, he hits the rock, slides down, and scratches his body back and forth in the process. He doesn't mind any of this, but he is very careful about one thing, namely, that no harm come to his right hand, which he is holding up. This is because he is balancing, on his pinkie, a little eagle the size of a matchbox, which is testing its wings with each leap. The eaglet's name is Oscar Peterson. For one instant, the rock-rover glimpses a pair of train track rails running into the infinite in the great heat. He kneels on the ground, puts his ear on the rail, and starts to listen, but in the sunlight the sparkling steel is burning hot, so he cannot orient his ear properly.

In the meantime, an apple-sized and true-to-life model of the globe begins to orbit around his head, naturally also rotating around its own axis. As he brings his head closer to the track, inevitably the orbiting planet also touches the rail. When the oceans come close to the metal, the splashing crested waves spout up like sizzling steam, and when the mountain peaks approach, they scratch against the rail, making sparks. Meanwhile Peterson, the little eaglet on Clint's shoulder, dips his beak with great gusto into the water of the large rivers' waters as they approach him, to relieve his thirst.

Experimental Effects and Scenery

Even in its early period, the band applied various experimental effects at concerts. The primary goal was to boost musical intuition and the production's effect. However, it had such an elemental impact on the entire production that, along with this, it greatly enhanced the suggestion. In the beginning there was no reverb yet; that is, there were no possibilities for echo settings for the vocals, nor for other sound effects. For this reason we used the simple method of simultaneously recording and playing a given sound with a multi-head Akai tape recorder. The staggered arrangement of the tape player heads, which we could rely on even when the tape speed changed, provided a woozy echo. Imagine this at that time when instruments were played through tube amplifiers, without mixing boards. The experimental effects came into being along with the echo. We recorded various natural and animal sounds in wildlife and at zoos. Since at that time there were still no accessible electronic sound libraries, we made them ourselves. We recorded various church bell ringings and slowed them down; later we purchased bells. We reworked the pre-recorded sounds with the tape recorder, putting a time shift on it, that is, echo and other noises, so that they would fit the archaic flood of images that we had imagined in advance for the concert. Of course these were not activated at the beginning of the concert; rather, we turned them on during the music performance, when the involvement had already taken shape (on the band's and audience's part), which almost automatically advanced the creation of the stage music. This experimental supporting effect gave plasticity to the internal picturing that accompanied our music. It was as if we were gliding through a temporally and spatially infinite medium, accompanied by sounds and music, where the accompanying images appeared plastically. We slowed the recorded animal sounds substantially, and played it like this along with the music. This brought a special floating quality to the musical passage which generated further intuitions. On the band's first album, whale sounds supported the improvisational parts. We produced similar interesting effects for our ritual theater performances so that we could intensify the dreamy effect.

At a few concerts, at the stunning parts, I had the guitars make sounds with a condenser microphone, To achieve a delay, we connected them to the tape recorder. With the microphone I strummed the strings, and the tape recorder played the sounds back with a delay. Thus we were able to achieve a kind of floating delay effect that professional pedals could not accomplish at that time. We used similar amplification for the special sounding of the bassist's violin.

In the 1980s, we made use of a kettledrum, two of them, which we amplified and tuned to the normal drum kit. We had a separate kettle drummer. Rhythm was a basic element for our ecstatic music.

The recordings of the concerts seemed quite interesting, but came nowhere close to conveying the suggestive effect that arose on site. During the concert, a special resonance was created in the room as a result of the sound waves, the crowd's spiritual force, and the energy radiating from the band members. Even today, science cannot precisely explain the working mechanism of this resonance; we can only describe its effect approximately. One thing is for sure: during a successful concert, an altered state of consciousness took hold in both the band and the audience. Of course, not in everyone to the same degree, but according to friends' reports, the less sensitive audience members also experienced some kind of interesting effect.

As time went on, we not only applied experimental effects, but tried making sounds with different kinds of objects, equipping them with pick-ups and then making sounds with them at the very moments during the music-building when we felt the need. Naturally we had to take care that the sounds not jolt us out of the concert experience and internal music-creation. These sound-making objects were, for example, large empty cupboards, into which we strung bass strings crosswise: strumming these, and amplifying the sound, produced a stunning effect. A similarly inspiring experience was produced by sounding a 1.1 x 2 meter steel sheet, which we did by holding it vertically and shaking it; the sound effect could be compared to a storm accompanying an earthquake. At a few of our concerts we installed a medium-sized copper bell on a giant carpentered wooden stand, which we microphoned and played during the concert by pulling it with a cord, while adding a large echo and delay to it. At our concerts we used similar devices as well: pipes, iron, whose arsenal I shall not enumerate here.

A close friend of ours, a graphic artist, who also drew many of our posters, worked quite creatively in planning and preparing our stage designs. Among other designs, this consisted of archaic symbols painted onto a large screen, which meant not only copying the symbols, but also transforming them into works of art. Besides this, the theatrical spatial scenery that came out of his hands fit the mood and experience of the concerts in a striking and inspiring way. The decorative scenery elements, assembled from natural materials and suspended over the stage, became an indispensable part of our concerts. We also took care to situate these brilliant decorations appropriately, in a way that would have an effect and receive good lighting. We had some concerts in which, behind and above the band, an enormous figure made of beef shank bones hung on a cord, as if this beast were trying to step onto the audience. We transported the bones there from the slaughterhouse in the trunk of a Trabant with the seats removed, in several trips. With good lighting, the scenery was quite effective, intensified by the suspended bones' movement during the concert; the whole figure swayed behind us and above our heads.

A famous American band that played after us announced that they had never seen such original scenery in their lives.

A memorable concert experience is also associated with a stage image in which, above the stage, a beam of light, swaying back and forth, shone through a street lampshade suspended from the ceiling on a long cord. We set this lamp in motion during the concert, and the music, together with the swaying light, created a terrific effect.

At our concerts we always went through a kind of spiritual transformation. This experience was combined with our internal need, taking shape imperceptibly, to use various costumes and masks supporting the musical performance art, as well as other props, decorations, or devices that intensified the sound effect.

A famous Hungarian art film shows an excerpt of one of our concerts, in which there was an enormous net in the background of the stage, suspended in such a way that in ecstatic situations one could leap and swing in it. This recording was made in the Mátyásföld neighborhood, in the Ikarus House of Culture. Among other happenings at that time, the concert associated with the film recording was big news; other bands also played there that night. Preparing for the concert, we made deep and comprehensive agreements with each other and the director, in which we worked out the performance process and its images that we wanted to transmit from within, extending to every detail. We bombarded each other with motivating stories and their effects, striving to make this as vivid and cathartic an experience as possible. This could be paired with a stunning experience, or to the contrary, it could be a woozy and bawdy scene in which we would fall over laughing. We left it so that utterly spontaneous ideas and happenings would arise. We wanted to bring this about in the music, just as in the performance art. Of course, we didn't want to do all this in an artificial environment and according to rehearsal, but in its own reality and spontaneity. My own costume was as follows: wearing a bathing suit, I had a bucket of honey poured over me from head to toe, and sandals made of compressed newspaper were tied with string to my feet. A tremendous wig was placed on my head, and when it was ready, I was strewn with a cascade of feathers from a down pillow. In this costume I ran onto the stage; racing around wildly, I started the concert with our drummer. Our singer arrived with a huge, twenty-four-kilo watermelon; he initiated his stage appearance by cutting a big opening in the melon, pulling it over his head, and running onstage. Of course he couldn't see a thing, the melon's red juice spurted out onto his white shirt and pants, its weight pulling his head down. Swaying as a result, then ecstatically jumping headlong, he burst onto the stage, knocking down a few microphone stands and control boxes. This caused the melon to break in two, his head cracked, and blood mixed with the red of the melon's juice. Our bass guitarist, responding to the cathartic effect, charged toward the net and leaped into it, swung in it, then jumped next to our singer. All of this can seem a little bit strange and laughable when told in this way, but it gave the psychedelic music and performance art on stage an entirely different effect, as this concert audience reciprocated by experiencing the dimensions that reflect the challenges of the unknown world. These quick events happened so suddenly and unexpectedly that the director neglected to start the recording, which the camera operator started only after these events. Afterwards they told us that this had had such an overwhelming effect on them that, paralyzed, they just watched the happenings on stage. Thus the most cathartic part was left out of the film. Namely, in this case we had unequivocally insisted on spontaneity and unrepeatability.

Another film captured one of our concerts almost in its entirety. Here we agreed to the recording on the condition that we give the concert in its full natural state, without interruption or any kind of conformity to the demands of the film. From the ceiling we suspended a wooden wagon wheel with iron rims; from the wheel we hung steel pipes of various thicknesses and lengths, along with other iron objects that made various sounds. To the center of the wheel we attached a field microphone that picked up the clanging sounds, which we then played, amplified with echo, along with the concert music. The extraordinarily effective ringing and rolling sound-flow of the pipes and iron objects, resounding alongside the ecstatic jumps and leaps, provided the basic dynamic of the concert. They all reinforced each other: the ecstatic movements, the resulting sound effects, and the music influenced by it all. This time, our singer put on a vest made out of a fishing net with a large carp thrashing in it, and moved ecstatically around, below, or above the clanging chariot wheel. Our bass guitarist sometimes jumped onto the swaying wheel played while swinging on it and kicking the pipes around.

I would have liked, with all of this, to allow the reader to imagine the cathartic effect of our performance-art music creation, as well as the magic of transformation, intensified by the scenery and our costume-like outfits. The atmosphere created by the music and the performance had a mystical effect that shattered the barriers of the mind through spiritual transfiguration. This is one of the reasons why we felt such an inner urge to advance and motivate a kind of inner transformation that helped this mystical effect to take place.

Perhaps this is why, in support of the performance art, we used various scenery items and our own handmade costumes: in other words, outer layers that transformed us into new and different personalities.

The Ritual Movement Theater

I will begin by saying that in the initial period we went to Lake Balaton in the summers to have fun. At one point we discovered that we could get a few things from the theater costume rental, and with these we traveled out to the lakeside.

Essentially, we rented king and page costumes, with fitting shoes and other supplements. We put all of this into a large black lacquered suitcase, and set out on our way in the strangest costumes. We had a long-haired friend with strong glasses, a theoretical physics student, who pulled a rubber swimming cap onto his head and joined the team like this. Someone might show up with a thick fake mustache and beret, or else with bathing gear (striped swimming trunks with side fastening) pulled onto his head. This is how the team headed off by train in the great summer heat. Our first trip took us to Siófok, to the Golden Coast open beach, where, in front of amazed bathers, pulling out items from the huge lacquered suitcase, the strangely attired people dressed up the king and pages. In the meantime, terribly good music blasted from the battery-powered tape player, which we always took with us. Within moments, an enormous crowd gathered around our troupe; especially the GDR tourists gazed daydreamingly at the beach happenings. They might have thought we were some traveling circus show. After dressing, the team entered the water with clothes on. The king went in front, his royal robe floating on the surface of the water; behind him, the pages and the other variously dressed attendants followed. In the meantime, the pages poured out drinks and served them on a tray. Of course this was quite difficult in the water, so sometimes they went underwater with the trays. This was a defining experience for me, and I think for the others too. Thus an outer shell, transforming us into other personalities, assists the liberation of internal spiritual experiences and allows us to cast away everyday limits. I think ancient rituals may have been formed in a similar manner and similarly exerted their effect.

Influenced by these and similar experiences, our company of friends created a ritual movement theater based on more serious principles and ancient mythological elements. Here friendship and internal spiritual connection united the participants, among whom, along with the girls' teamwork and force, some boys turned up as stalwart members and made the shows quite effective. Already after the first performances, a Danish avant-garde theater director (a woman) oversaw their workings. She helped create the first few shows. After this, the girls worked independently.

For me, theater was always one of the important accompanying elements of musical performance, mobilizing the spiritual effect and its force field. Archaic three-dimensional images, together with the musical current born there at that moment, brought a special atmosphere and energy field into being. The emerging effect, zigzagging between the souls, created a regenerating experience, which was transmitted to everyone in the form of a shared cascade of emotion.

This was actually the kind of ritual movement theater in which mythological elements and stories were reworked and used with predilection. It invoked, for instance, different folk customs, nature and fertility festivals, mythological thought systems and festive circles.

Along with movement, scenery and dress ornaments dominated. The girls reworked the given story, and to display the images belonging to it, made the various costumes and stage designs in the most realistic way, with their own hands; the basic materials came from flea markets.

The main source for such materials was the Ecseri market, which functioned as Budapest's largest used item market, even then. The girls went there with predilection and obtained the most extreme thingamabobs, odds and ends, from which headdresses and various costume-creations were later born.

Among the used materials there were even dry twigs, hay, various kinds of fiber, bones, plants, litterfall, seeds, and flowers. Our graphics friend, who also made our album covers and posters, excelled at planning the stage scenery. The decorations were displays of natural and archaic objects and images that organically fit the given performance. In the performances, the display of the four ancient elements played a large role.

The initial team of four or five girls was later supplemented. There were two quite ambitious guys who, as professional cavers, knew the safe methods of suspension and were able to apply them. They worked out the scenes played in the air, when, for example, in a hall you had to slide down from a 15-20-meter-high ceiling or fly into or out of the audience. Nor did they shy away when a king with bird wings and human shape, hanging from an immense hall ceiling, had to abduct the Spring Fairy above the heads of the crowd.

The other participants are important to mention, since they played an enormous role in the preparation of various masks and headdresses; in fact, they deserve a tip of the hat. The theater shows were similar to an art performance but resembled nothing that had been seen in Hungary up to that time. They also had the important characteristic of being played among the audience, in the crowd, on the ground, in the air. Various suspended structures and props supporting the play's message functioned both as scenery and as tools for use. Important elements of the theater performance were the podiums set up at different points in the space, which the actors, moving among the crowd and providing the story's continuity, approached in a special procession, then, in sync, joined the messages into a unified story. The marchers were joined by the crowd, who increasingly desired to take part in the story. On the podiums, among decorations consisting of ancient altars and various archaic motifs, the story's central sayings were displayed.

Light technique supported and accompanied the movement. Moving reflectors and colored lights provided the appropriate effect. There was a performance where fire-breathers and torch-bearing dancers appeared descending on a rope bridge and completed the mythological story with their ecstatic dance.

An important accompaniment to the theatrical piece was the music, which several members of the band played spontaneously when hit by inspiration during the show. The music's task was to accompany the stage story, based on intuition that the story had generated. This was supported by sound effects that were likewise matched to the story and which we had produced in advance. A very good friend of ours, a technician, took care of starting the effects at the right times during the story, fitting them to the actions, and playing them. The theatrical and musical performance realized in this manner became a unique production. It is no accident that the theater was invited with the band, among others, to one of the most prestigious western European alternative artistic festivals, where they performed together one evening with the Catalan theatrical group La Fura dels Baus. The festival was held in the Tempodrom of what was still West Berlin, in a huge circus tent, which fit about 2,500 to 3,000 people.

In 1987, during the Amsterdam art weeks, at the personal intercession of Queen Beatrix of the Netherlands, the Hungarian authorities allowed the theater to travel together with the band; originally they would have sent others instead, but even so, we could list performances that have taken place in truly prestigious venues and have been recognized abroad. Unfortunately, in the case of the theater, the media reaction was similar to that received by the band; that is, the Hungarian media made no mention of their activities, neither then nor now. This despite the fact that it gave sold-out shows for several thousand viewers and was a defining group in the alternative artistic palette. In contrast, the foreign press always announced their shows and highlighted their unique and unconventional performance style. In the magazine *GEO Special*, in an issue devoted to Budapest, a multi-page article appeared, with photos, about one of their sold-out shows at home, emphasizing its level and extraordinary effect.

As with the concerts, two identical productions were never prepared or performed. The shared performances happened in such a way that the theater started the evening, and then at the end of the piece, in a continuous procession, without an intermission, the concert began.

If I had to summarize the essence of the ritual movement theater, I would perhaps highlight the summoning of archaic mythological elements, which made for a shared ceremony-like event, in which the audience, too, was inspired to live out the piece. Thus everyone could feel like a creator of and contributor to the performed story. All of this took place in a space that displayed a dreamlike, vision-like world, where the audience could take part actively in the mythological event. For a video and photos of the ritual movement theater, use this QR code:

This plastically displayed performance mode shaped free internal picturing into realistic images, a visual image stream, which, with its light and sound effects, enabled the experience of internal spiritual events. This show and performance art, created together with the band, perhaps gave the most dimension to the internal experience, to a journey in which dream and reality could become one, the boundaries of past and present lost their significance, and the experience of archaic images produced a cathartic effect that evoked everyone's common involvement—that is, joy for all. Thus not only the performers and musicians zigzagging among the audience, but the audience itself became an organic part of the happenings and experience that we lived out together. This performance mode broke completely with the usual theatrical customs up to that time, in which well-dressed people in comfortable seats clap tastefully at the end of a piece because that is the custom. Here everyone could do what they felt like. Already within the first seconds everything suggested this, as a stream of group experiences began in the concert hall along with the stream of music. The feeling of infinite freedom swept quickly over everyone, and the power of shared experience filled the entire space.

The Working Principle of Mass Hypnosis

If we understand our brain's working principles, we become capable of handling and warding off the damaging effects of soul-destroying mass hypnosis applied insidiously today through advertising campaigns and other means. One may ask: if only positive energies can be activated with hypnosis, how is today's anti-human, media-induced mass hypnosis even possible? The explanation is that the kinds of outward beauty, convenience, and good life imposed on us through powerful visual bombardment are equated with happiness, through the virtually transmitted, false, induced bewitchment of idols. This is the virtual state of happiness, which generates a false internal function and an erroneous notion, thereby eliminating one of the primary functions of our brain. This primary function—as I mentioned earlier—is nothing other than our brain's internal picturing capacity, which our creativity depends on. We must understand that true and real positive spiritual energy cannot come about through virtual networks.

A defining element of the band's work was the mutual transfer of suggestions during music creation. The realization, during the music, of visual apparitions created a meditative atmosphere among the band members. These states' subjective aspect diverged more and more from the everyday. In the suggestive atmosphere induced by the music and performance, the usual environmental and social stimuli ceased. In this heightened state we could pay better attention to each other than during ordinary social contact, and thus everyone became more sensitive to each other's reactions. In this situation, almost immediately, ecstatic, involuntary synchronized movement was born. The same forms of behavior and action took shape in the audience as well. That is, the suggestions given by individual band members to each other, reinforced by the effect of shared music-making, were transferred to the listeners. Those taking part in the process executed more and more of the suggestions involuntarily, without any forcing of the will. Through the coordination achieved in this manner, the individual reactions became synchronized. In other words, during the music flow, a musician's internal spiritual state, inspiring a suggestion, became harmonized with the other musicians' and the audience's reactions. During music-creation, every further suggestion, arousing the intuition, was transmitted by different band members, according to how they were affected by the music flow, and the member receiving the strongest intuition at the moment provided the spark for the creation of common synchronization. Regarding intuition, it is important to note that it cannot be summoned by the will; it arises spontaneously. During a concert, this took the form of an unexpected sound and beat that came just at the right moment, not when we wanted it. Such is the magical creation of music.

The audience's involvement in the production was essential to us. For this, we had to come into a close spiritual relationship with each other, which we reached by exercising a certain concentration regularly, arms around each other, in a quiet place, before the start of the concert. This was similar to athletes' huddle before a match, at the end of which they emphasize their intentions with a shout. We then had to pass this synchronicity on to the crowd. In this state we became sensitive to the need, on the part of so many interested glances, open ears and souls, for their unsure vacillation to receive an answer and validation and become pure. Our lived images were activated, and flowing into the music, some special and strange effect swam in the air. Breathtaking experiences raced with unbridled ferocity on the waves of the music flow. An exceptional force came to life, which, together with the audience, we felt in our chests. The majestic wildness running through everyone and the pure sensual charge led everyone to feel that if they came close, they might not only catch fire, but actually burn. The howling and the intoxication of the trance, along with the waves of the musical sounds, brought everyone into its power, and the sense of the universe made them forget the limits of space and time. The usual styles and forms lost their validity in this journey. Everything became and seemed a given, everything had its own place, and everything found its place in the flow of the performance. A strange, pleasant feeling and spiritual liberty broke forth, causing a communal, infinite dash toward novelty and the world of the unknown; this enabled us to bring back the vanished, lost foundations of cultures and at the same time prepared us to create new worlds. In this state, music creation happens automatically. This in no way resembles the kind of improvisation applied in jazz; here the change of emotional bursts and spiritual waves affects the music, through the release of sounds motivated by internal images. A person feels that he is capable of almost anything. Every single sound, every sound-sliver has significance and a separate force field.

As a result of such tuning to each other, a temporarily powerful emotional bond was formed, which in scholarly literature is called archaic involvement. In this state, for instance, various emotional transferences play an essential role, as does the excavation of various archaic images. These further excite the nascent intuitive motivation and image-making.

The aforementioned mechanism already worked at a certain level when rock music emerged, or in the hippie world, where the ecstatic state and the accompanying mutual tuning and involvement were already known effects. Today's lifestyle fashion trends tend toward killing social connections. Self-realization is advertised with the goal of disorienting the young generation. The advertisers pour false concepts and soul-killing virtual glitz onto people, investing enormous sums of money in advertising and profit-making productions. As a result, in Western societies, more and more people struggle with mental problems and go to therapy in need of psychological help. The relationship with our souls and the fulfillment of our internal world, the need to discuss our spiritual problems with our loved ones and friends, has been nearly squeezed out of our modern-day rushed world, which puts our egos first. Because of this, we become enclosed in ourselves, carrying these hidden spiritual burdens solitarily in a mechanized, informatic, virtual world, where we chat with each other in abbreviations about completely average and superfluous things. Nonetheless, the generations growing up into adulthood have always needed archaic involvement, that is, family affection, the experience of true friendships and loves; the experience of the kind of involuntary synchronicity where new worlds can open up, the false, idol-worshipping outer world loses its significance, and the internal, true forces come to the surface. We often say about someone in love that he is "losing his head"; that is, the real outer world ceases to exist for him, and he sees just his beloved partner, with whom he lives out every moment. Similarly, true friend relationships, usually formed in youth, endure and bring about such a strong involvement that the friends are capable of doing everything for each other almost unconditionally. But the truly strongest involvement is the one that we experience in relation with our children and parents.

Thus hypnosis works in our normal lives between two or more people; that is, the suggestions are present at every level in everyday life, and to some degree nearly every person experiences the effect, since we live in society and human relationships fill our lives. The modern era tries to kill these naturally working social relationships. Since youth is still more sensitive to true and pure internal matters, it seeks an escape from this treadmill. Many reach for drugs and alcohol, hoping to find what they are missing, that is, those things that differ from the external, cold world and that could complete their internal, spiritual world. The key lies not in substitutes, however, but in the development of social relationships, in the strongest possible recognition, experience, and development of our internal world completed by family, friendship, and love, and in true creation, drawing on the enchanted, magical knowledge dormant within us. This we can call the activation of a natural hypnotic relationship system, which through various suggestions can be realized during our lives. However, for the activation, it doesn't hurt to recognize and apply the process based on ancient transcendent knowledge, which means experiencing the kind of spiritual encounter which, through the radiation of faith, affects the working of the soul, so that it is capable of transforming and working an effect between people, without words.

Scholarly literature confirms the fact that mass hypnosis and trance-inducing processes were integral parts of various cultures' rituals. The enduring tradition, and the application today as hypnosis, of altered states of consciousness throughout the centuries proves that it is important to grapple with hypnosis today and to find the essence of the age-old tradition.

The atmosphere attained at our concerts released everyone's blocking stimuli in such a way that their behavior control progressively disappeared. The intensifying trance state made everyone capable of experiencing the emotional needs and body signals that were suppressed in a normal state. This triggered movement characteristic of a trance state among the audience members itself, which actually had happened earlier in the world at rock and pop concerts. As inhibitions vanished, new experiences and modes of behavior came into being, and new vistas opened, which the internal images fortified with the help of musical performance art.

When we bring another person (or ourselves) into hypnosis, a condition is mutual acceptance, profound trust felt toward each other, and the designation of a common goal, which can only be positive and forward-looking, regardless of the situation. This clearly came about at our concerts, since, arm in arm with our audience, we set out for an unknown world that appeared as a common but unnamable goal. The strange tension before the step into the unknown created a trustful relationship that endowed everyone with spiritual strength. In that state, both we and our audience attained relaxation, the quieting of spasms, relief from fear and pain, or the intensification of the force of the inner "I" itself.

The fact that not only the young generation was represented at our concerts, but older age groups as well, signified to us that we were able to embrace and set in motion a wide emotional spectrum that could affect people regardless of their age.

Another important perspective, which I would like to emphasize, is that today's young people would rather take part in parties, although such productions, alien to life and involving musical trance only, do not offer any kind of noetic challenge or soul-moving effect. Partying lacks wonder, which, fed from within, works its effect, providing noetic and spiritual energy for our soul. I believe that for this reason, among others, young people reach for drugs and other consciousness-altering substances. Nonetheless, I find that a certain layer of this generation seeks out productions that instead uphold noetic values and stimulate spiritual energies. Evidence of this can be found in unplugged concerts and the increasing number of live performances where this effect can be felt.

In the following pages I will try to describe the effect mechanism with which, during concerts, we could summon an altered state of consciousness, both on our own and with those members of the audience who received the suggestions. At such times, in the audience, noetic suggestibility increases, along with the easily inducible imitation of forms of behavior, which fortifies the effect of the altered state, according to our experience. This resulted in a substantial increase in suggestive influence. My internal images, which I lived out in a transformed state with the music and a special experience of travel, were transmitted to the audience as if by magic. But this effect mechanism worked within the band as well, between the members, since we were at once each other's mediums and sources of suggestion. Actually a spiritual confluence took place, which, arising from every moment of the incipient music stream and from the mutual imitation of images, reinforced us all emotionally. This on its own created a favorable medium for any suggestion. These were actually the musical junctions that we had set in image in advance—which we had captured before the concerts. In the crowd, the group spirit became quite defined, generating such a feeling of togetherness that it directed the individuals' will toward suggestions, affecting their emotions and imagination. It is no accident that after our 1984 concert in West Berlin, viewers reported on the very same internal experiences and images that we had had. In this concert, one of our most cathartic, representatives of the West-Berlin artistic world took part, as did representatives of the new wave and punk tendencies, but this varied audience included other layers of youth as well. During this concert, when particular images switched, the audience expressed its enthusiasm with special sound effects; later, at the end of the concert, when we put down the instruments, a speechless silence took hold for a few minutes, and only the hum of the feedback-thrumming guitars could be heard. Then a huge burst of applause broke out, and the crowd wanted to bring us back to the stage. From this and similar concerts the band gained fame both at home and abroad. At the heart of these situations was the fact that pure and unmanipulated forces have the most archaic and profound effect. This derives from our personality as well, since at that moment when we have to manipulate someone falsely in some way, or they try to manipulate us, the effect weakens. Our biology signals this, in fact, independently of our consciousness. We need only consider our body's various signals in tense situations. Experience lived out together, in a crowd, has an uplifting power, and brain function occurring on the communal plane has its particular effect mechanisms. Special and seemingly unbelievable forces come into being, which sometimes contradict our world built on everyday empirical experience and bounded by logical means.

According to scholarly literature, one of the characteristic attributes of the crowd is that it wishes immediately to realize and live out the received images, suggestions, or instructions. At our concerts, emotions increasingly led the way, motivated by the dynamic and cathartic musical transitions. The oneness of the received experiences and the noetic oscillations intensified the effect that audience members had on each other. The transfer of image-like experiences along with the musical performance art resulted in a plastic apparition. At the moment when a spark of the image-like experience bounced onto the listeners, the rest of the image stream, along with the experience, became a shared treasure, and the shared ardor swept up the uncertain, even skeptical audience members as well. The spark was lit by the image-making generated by our internal suggestions and the accompanying transformation. This was nothing other than the application and realization of transcendent knowledge. In that state, our brain is used more fully and effectively, with the activation of the right hemisphere. This can transport us to the province of relativistic time perception, which I wrote about earlier.

The question always was this: what is this carrier material, which triggers, induces, activates this collective experience? I saw, knew, and believed that something in the room zigzagged on the plane of thought, thus it must be some kind of force. At first I didn't want to believe that something like that could work. This elemental force is nothing other than mass suggestion. I knew that we as a band saw something in common, and this was truly a good feeling, but I was skeptical that we could pass it onward to others, that is, the audience. Then we reached the point where we believed in it, and we ascended the stage with the attitude that here is the crowd, and they have to feel and see it too, and we will be able to do this! This truly made it possible for us merely to toss a spark out over the heads of the crowd; that was enough for a stream to take off, which we often called flow-music.

When at a concert we could convey a series of images, that is, when we could plastically bring the crowd to imagine it, then faith and the realization tendency received a strong impetus. At such time the effect evoking the opposite force is quite small, so the crowd is easily influenced. Suddenly, the spark in the audience exploded with a domino effect. The shared enthusiasm swept the skeptical along with it, fulfilling their own visual thought process as well as their spiritual involvement.

It follows from the above that it is impossible to fake such a concert or not take it seriously, since that would mean the failure of the entire production. That certain spark had to bounce for the effect described above to come into being and work.

Actually it is my conviction that a truly deep and soul-moving artistic performance exerts its effect on the basic of such principles.

To sum up: that "carrier material" that triggers the collective experience is nothing other than the soul. The function of the soul affects our entire radiating energy and behavior, and is capable of affecting others with its force. We can stimulate our souls into motion by applying transcendent knowledge that our ancestors left behind; with this we can tap its dormant power. This we can attain with our brain's internal picturing and by joining our action with our faith. An internal process built and applied in such a way is capable of triggering effective suggestions and evoking the kind of collective experience that truly becomes enduring. The relationship of our heart and soul assures the unfurling of the experience and its completion through love.

Here I would like to refer back to the noetic force of communal, ceremonial prayers mentioned earlier. Our ancestors left us this ritual. It is no accident that these ceremonies happened in this way, involving the crowd in a shared experience, a shared noetic force field. A simple example is when we see a very good play, with good actors, which by its effect of involvement produces emotional eruptions in the audience. However, this works just there, at the location, not when we watch it again on film. In this case, the essential aspect is the communal involvement, which generates a brain function taking place for the sake of a common goal. This bombards our soul to varying degrees, depending on the effect and speed of the received images. The spiritual force field is capable of intensifying the experience according to the principle of resonance, and in certain cases the visual and emotional impulses communicated by the brain, which trigger a trance state, with which we can take part in the illusion. This is because faith in the image apparition mobilizes the soul's functioning. The more powerful the emotions that the image effect can transmit, the stronger this mobilization will be. This process evokes a special mental state, which can be a hallucination-generating process or a trance state. In such a state, not only does the brain's blood supply change significantly, through which the brain's function is intensified, but other physiological changes appear that are worthy of attention.

In the band's true golden era, in the fully improvisational and ecstatic parts of our performances, on many occasions, both our singer and I experienced automatic speech generation as a consequence of this type of trance state. I could describe this as actually the expression, with words or sounds, of internal spiritual happenings generated by the emotions. When playing back and listening to concerts we had recorded on tape, we concluded that the content and image-world of our automatic speech generation greatly resembled ancient shaman singing. Every ancient culture has left behind some kind of altered state of consciousness, institutionalized in the manner of the time and realized at a magical or sacral level. These rituals were naturally performed in community, and they endowed these ceremonies with great significance.

The well-applied arsenal of ecstatic drums and semitones enhances the experience and the effect. In such a state one need not concentrate on pre-written lyrics; we need only believe in the internal images and reflect them back, then diffuse and radiate them in the souls' energy field.

I have also thought about how, with the preceding explanations, I have given an explanation of individual spiritual and transcendent working mechanisms as well. The key to the secret is the heightened relativistic brain function and the special accompanying physiological changes. A kind of state can be reached where the hallucination or vision, brought about with the lived images, exerts its effect in a real way. Naturally at such a time everyone watches the same film and is convinced that it is reality. Here I would refer back to the Far-Eastern fakir stunts, which those standing around him experienced as a true occurrence, while he just sat in one place and told a story, yet, by carrying out the impeccable illusion, induced perfect involvement in the viewers.

We can differentiate a truly suggestive experience from a manipulated suggestion in that artificially forced matters do not stimulate our soul and heart; along with this, the magic of the experienced internal joy and collective encounter is missing. We should always listen to our soul and let our heart see, in the way that our ancestors have shown us. Things without soul are empty and cheap; that is, they do not offer a deep and enduring experience. Consider advertising campaigns or today's celebrity world: these are manipulated, short-lived and powerless experiments compared to true and deep, powerful and pure matters that emerge from the soul.

Conclusion

Life is a great adventure, promising many wonders. We would all like to experience and live this. I believe that in the band's golden era we were able to realize and experience this with the greatest effectiveness and pass it on to our audience. In that era, perhaps the stormiest feeling for me was that of limitless freedom and the magic of creation, which gave wings to our souls even in a system where it was prohibited even to think of democracy.

From the perspective of so much time, I can grasp the essence as follows: we do not always and every time have to convulsively insist on our fixed notions; instead, let us be open, let us dare to experience the infinite, the unknowable, with all its magic. Let us dare to activate our childhood fantasy. With such a mindset, nothing can force or limit us, nothing can take our freedom away. With this attitude, we can experience infinite freedom in our soul, since at such times we are unbound; this will bring about our definite boundless experience of happiness.

If, during a creative process, we start to plan, insist, or conform, at that moment we lose our internal freedom, since at such times we try to satisfy those strictures. If we are not able to discard these tendencies at once, then if life demands something different of us—perhaps we receive a new and stunning experience at a concert, or a creative idea strikes us— and we cannot, dare not receive the newer thing, this gives us the feeling that we are not free.

This means that we do not lose our freedom when life forces us to do something that we would rather not do, but even earlier, when we decided what we will willingly do and what we will not.

The most effective way to win back our internal spiritual freedom is by striving to become open to everything and releasing, giving up the conveniences we experience in the real world and the limits that give us a sense of safety. By achieving freedom, our soul can take wing, and thus our noetic energies can become the shapers of our lives. This way, our mind has the opportunity to scan the paths of the infinite, and drawing from this, to arouse a true authentic life-shaping force through mobilization of our soul. The harmony of our soul and heart will not disappoint us; it is capable of stimulating our energies and multiplying our brain capacities and abilities with the power of love. By applying magical, ancient, transcendent knowledge, that is, bringing our soul to life, we will be able to originate new things, to create, and, along with this, to transmit our internal energy to others, that is, to exert an effect. Thus the carrier energy is the soul itself. During our life it is important to recognize the talent that we were born with and to have the courage to draw on it, since this truly draws on the soul.

Again and again, exceptional, successful people—athletes, scientists, artists, or people attaining significant results in other areas, people who do their work obsessively—are asked what drives them. The essence of their answers is usually that the magic of the alternation of valleys (failures) and peaks (successes) experienced during their work propels them forward.

However, the experience of unlimited spiritual freedom and its impact is actually the driving force that can influence our lives and the lives of others.

In conclusion, I would just like to say that to those who succeeded in understanding and living out, or perhaps just feeling the secret hiding in the lines of this book, I wish them the wonder of life as they continue forward on their path!

References

Zimbardo, Philip, and Nikita D. Coulombe. *Man (Dis)connected.*
Rider/Ebury Publishing (UK), 2015.

Tepperwein, Kurt. *Die hohe Schule der Hypnose.* Geneva: Ariston
Verlag, 1977.

THE AUTHOR

Sándor Czakó was born in 1957 in Budapest, Hungary, where he grew up, attended school, and studied classical guitar. He graduated from the Technical University of Budapest in nuclear engineering and subsequently obtained a Ph.D. degree. After working for several years as an engineering researcher, he started his own engineering consultancy company, of which he is the managing director. In 1973, during his last years of high school, he and his fellow musicians founded the band Vágtázó Halottkémek (Galloping Coroners); he remained a core member until 1989 and continued working with the ritual theater into the early 1990s. The band's golden era had a great influence on him and the band's followers. During that time, besides making music, he became fascinated with musical experimentation and the effect of music on audiences. In recent years he has taken great interest in the psychology of art, particularly the effects of music on our brain function, which he has tried to interpret and relate to his experiences with Galloping Coroners. He continues to dedicate his life to freedom, creation, art, and science.

THE TRANSLATOR

Diana Senechal is the 2011 winner of the Hiett Prize in the Humanities and the author of two books of nonfiction, *Republic of Noise* (2012) and *Mind over Memes* (2018), the poetry collection *Solo Concert* (Serving House Books, 2025), and numerous stories, essays, songs, and translations. Her new book, *More and Less Than a Friend: The Songwriting Partnership of Tamás Cseh and Géza Bereményi in Hungary*, will be published by Serving House Books in 2026. Since 2017 she has been living and teaching in Szolnok, Hungary. For more about her work, see dianasenechal.com.

www.ingramcontent.com/pod-product-compliance
Lightning Source LLC
Chambersburg PA
CBHW021329060726

47591CB00006B/1940